THE NEW WINDMILL SERIES

General Editors: Anne and Ian Serraillier

75

THE WHEEL ON THE SCHOOL

The children of a little school in a Dutch fishing village want to entice back the storks who used to roost on the roof. And what storks like, they discover, is a wheel. They set out to find one and, though sometimes everything seems to be against them, they don't give up until they succeed. 'A quaintly illustrated, natural and beautifully told story, full of suspense . . . It would be a fine basis for a primary school project on Holland.'—*The Use of English*

MEINDERT DeJONG

The Wheel
on the School

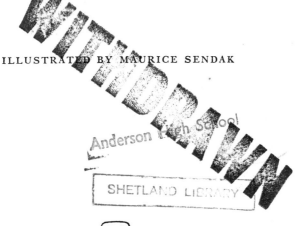

ILLUSTRATED BY MAURICE SENDAK

HEINEMANN EDUCATIONAL BOOKS
LONDON

Heinemann Educational Books Ltd
22 Bedford Square, London WC1B 3HH

LONDON   EDINBURGH   MELBOURNE   AUCKLAND
HONG KONG   SINGAPORE   KUALA LUMPUR   NEW DELHI
IBADAN   NAIROBI   JOHANNESBURG   KINGSTON
EXETER (NH)   PORT OF SPAIN

ISBN 0 435 12075 1

First published in Great Britain 1956 by Lutterworth Press
First published in the New Windmill Series 1964
Reprinted 1966, 1968, 1971, 1973, 1976,
1979

Printed in Great Britain
by Butler & Tanner Ltd, Frome and London

CONTENTS

To my nieces
Shirley and Beverly
And their flying fingers

CHAPTER I

Do You Know About Storks?

To START with there was Shora. Shora was a fishing village in Holland. It lay on the shore of the North Sea in Friesland, tight against the dike. Maybe that was why it was called Shora. It had some houses and a church and tower. In five of those houses lived the six school children of Shora, so that is important. There were a few more houses, but in those houses lived no children—just old people. They were, well, just old people, so they weren't too important. There were more children, too, but young children, toddlers, not school children—so that is not so important either.

The six children of Shora all went to the same little school. There was Jella; he was the biggest of the six. He was big and strong for his age. There was Eelka. He was slow and clumsy, except his mind; his mind was swift. There was Auka, and right here at the

1

beginning there is nothing much to say about Auka
—he was just a nice, everyday boy. You could have
fun with him. There were Pier and Dirk; they were
brothers. Pier and Dirk looked about as much alike as
second cousins. But Pier liked what Dirk liked, and
Dirk did what Pier did. They liked to be together.
They were twins.

Then there was Lina. She was the only girl in the
little Shora school. One girl with five boys. Of course,
there was also a teacher, a man teacher.

Maybe to begin with, we really should have started
with Lina. Not because she was the only schoolgirl
in Shora, but because she wrote a story about storks.
There were no storks in Shora. Lina had written this
story about storks of her own accord—the teacher
hadn't asked her to write it. In fact, until Lina read it
out loud to the five boys and the teacher, nobody in
school had even thought about storks.

But there one day, right in the middle of the
arithmetic lesson, Lina raised her hand and asked,
'Teacher, may I read a little story about storks? I
wrote it all myself, and it's about storks.'

Lina called it a story, but it was really an essay, a
composition. The teacher was so pleased that Lina had
written a little piece of her own accord, he stopped the
arithmetic lesson there and let Lina read her story.
She began with the title and read on:

DO YOU KNOW ABOUT STORKS?

Do you know about storks? Storks on your roof bring all
kinds of good luck. I know this about storks; they are big and
white and have long yellow bills and tall yellow legs. They
build great big messy nests, sometimes right on your roof. But
when they build a nest on the roof of a house, they bring good
luck to that house and to the whole village that that house
stands in. Storks do not sing. They make a noise like you do
when you clap your hands when you feel happy and good.
I think storks clap their bills to make the happy sounds
when they feel happy and good. They clap their bills almost

2

all the time except when they are in the marshes and ditches hunting for frogs and little fishes and things. Then they are quiet. But on your roof they are noisy. But it is a happy noise, and I like happy noises.

That is all I know about storks; but my aunt in the village of Nes knows a lot about storks, because every year two big storks come to build their nest right on her roof. But I do not know much about storks, because storks never come to Shora. They go to all the villages all around, but they never come to Shora. That is the most that I know about storks, but if they came to Shora, I would know more about storks.

After Lina had finished reading her story, the room was quiet. The teacher stood there looking proud and pleased. Then he said, 'That was a fine story, Lina. A very fine composition, and you know quite a lot about storks!' His eyes were pleased and bright. He turned to big Jella. 'Jella,' he said, 'what do you know about storks?'

'About storks, Teacher?' Jella said slowly. 'About

storks—nothing.' He looked surly and stubborn, because he felt stupid. He thought he ought to explain. 'You see,' he told the teacher, 'I can't bring them down with my catapult. I've tried and tried, but I just can't seem to do it.'

The teacher looked startled. 'But why would you want to shoot them down?'

'Oh, I don't know,' Jella said. He wriggled a little in his seat. He looked unhappy. 'Because they move, I suppose.'

'Oh,' the teacher said. 'Pier,' he said then, 'Dirk, what do you twins know about storks?'

'About storks?' Pier asked. 'Nothing.'

'Dirk,' the teacher said.

'Just the same as Pier,' Dirk said. 'Nothing.'

'Pier,' the teacher said, 'if I had asked Dirk first, what would have been your answer?'

'The same as Dirk's,' Pier answered promptly. 'Teacher, that's the trouble with being twins—if you don't know something, you don't know it double.'

The teacher and the room liked that. It made everybody laugh. 'Well, Auka,' the teacher said, 'how about you?'

Auka was still chuckling and feeling good about what Pier had said, but now he looked serious. 'All I know is that if storks make happy noises with their bills like Lina said in her story, then I would like storks, too.'

The teacher looked around and said: 'Well, Eelka, there in the corner, that leaves only you.'

Eelka thought awhile. 'I'm like Lina, Teacher; I know little about storks. But if storks would come to Shora, then I think I would learn to know a lot about storks.'

'Yes, that is true,' the teacher said. 'But now what do you think would happen if we all began to think a lot about storks? School's almost over for today, but if,

4

from now until tomorrow morning when you come back to school, you thought and thought about storks, do you think things would begin to happen?'

They all sat still and thought that over. Eelka raised his hand. 'But I'm afraid I can't think much about storks when I don't know much about storks. I'd be finished in a minute.'

Everybody laughed, but the teacher's eyes weren't pleased. 'True, true,' he said. 'That's right, Eelka. We can't think much when we don't know much. But we can wonder! From now until tomorrow morning when you come to school again, will you do that? Will you wonder why and wonder why? Will you wonder why storks don't come to Shora to build their nests on the roofs, the way they do in all the villages around? For sometimes when we wonder, we can make things begin to happen.

'If you'll do that—then school is over now!'

CHAPTER II

To Wonder Why

THERE they were out in the playground—free! Jella peered again over the roofs of the houses at the distant tower rising beside the dike. He couldn't believe it. But the big white face of the tower clock spelled out three—a little past three. 'Boy,' Jella said in wonderment, 'he let us out almost a whole hour early, just because of storks.' Jella was beginning to appreciate storks. 'What'll we do?' he said eagerly to the other boys.

But Lina took charge. Since she had started it with her essay about storks, she felt responsible. It was a wonderful day, the sky was bright and blue, the dike was sunny. 'Let's all go and sit on the dike and wonder why, just like the teacher said.'

Nobody objected. They all dutifully set out for the dike, still feeling happy because of this hour of freedom that had so suddenly and unexpectedly come to

6

them. Still grateful enough to the storks and Lina to be obedient to her and sit on the dike and think about storks. But Jella lagged behind, and that was unusual. Big Jella was generally in the lead. Going down the village street he stared at every house he passed as if they were something new in the new freedom. But he dutifully climbed the dike and dutifully sat down at the end of the row of boys. Lina sat at the other end.

They sat. Nobody seemed to know just how to begin to wonder without the teacher there to start them off. Jella stared up at the sky. There wasn't a cloud in the sky. There were no storks. There wasn't even a gull. Jella looked at the sea stretching empty before him—there wasn't a ship in the sea.

Jella looked along the quiet row. Everybody was just sitting, hugging his knees. Everybody looked quiet and awkward and uncomfortable. Suddenly Jella had had enough. He looked along the row of boys at Lina. 'The teacher didn't say we had to sit in a row on the dike to wonder, did he?'

'No,' Lina said, 'but I thought, well, he's never given us a whole hour off from school before, and I thought . . .'

'Well, then,' Jella said . . . It just didn't feel right to sit when you were free. But the quiet sea and the quiet sky suggested nothing to him. Then fortunately a slow canalboat came pushing around a faraway bend in the canal. The two men on deck lowered the sail and the mast, so the boat could slide under the low bridge. The men picked up poles to push the boat along under the bridge. Jella jumped up. Now he had an idea. 'Hey, let's all get our poles and go ditch jumping!'

All the boys, with the exception of Eelka, jumped up eagerly. Here was something to do—fun in the freedom.

7

'You, too, Eelka. Run and get your pole,' Jella said. 'And tell Auka to get mine, too. I'll wait here.'

Lina stared at Jella in dismay. Even Eelka had to go. When it came to ditch jumping, Eelka generally was left out—he was too fat and slow and clumsy. 'But I thought we were going to wonder why storks don't come to Shora?' Lina said. If even Eelka had to go along, she was going to be left behind all alone.

Lina glared down the dike after the running boys. 'All right for you, Eelka,' she yelled unhappily. She looked darkly at Jella. 'Boy, if the teacher finds out that you . . .' She swallowed her words. It was a bitter, lost feeling to be left behind all alone in the surprise free hour.

Lina had a sudden hopeful thought. It must be that Jella wanted them all in on the ditch jumping, so that if the teacher found out, they'd all catch it together. Maybe he'd let her in on it, too! Maybe that was why he had stayed here with her on the dike. 'Jella,' Lina asked, 'can I go, too? Why, if it wasn't for me, you'd be sitting in school right now. And I could get my mother's clothes pole. It's long and smooth and . . .'

'Naw,' Jella said immediately. 'Girls are no good at jumping. It's a boy's game.'

'I'd be just as good as Eelka. Better even,' Lina said indignantly.

'Yes, you would. But Eelka doesn't mind getting wet, but girls worry about wet feet and their dresses flying. And they squeal and scream, and then they get scared and go giggly.'

Jella seemed to have thought a lot about it. Lina could see it was totally no use wheedling or arguing. She drew her wooden shoes primly up under her, hugged her knees, and stared wretchedly out at the sea. 'Teacher said we were to wonder why the storks don't come. He even said if we wondered really hard things might began to happen.'

8

'We'll wonder while we jump ditches,' Jella said shortly. He was a bit uneasy. But now the boys were coming back, Auka with two vaulting poles. Jella started to leave. 'And we don't care if you do tell the teacher! He didn't say we were supposed to sit like dopes on the dike.'

So Jella did care—he was even worried she would tell. She was no telltale! Lina did not deign to turn around to answer. But she couldn't help looking down the dike when Eelka came dragging his long vaulting pole. 'All right for you, Eelka,' she said stormily.

That was the trouble with being the only girl: you got left out of things. And if Eelka didn't also get left out, there was nothing for her to do but sit by herself or play with her little sister Linda and the other little children. What was the fun of that? Well, she'd show them. She'd sit right here and think and wonder really hard. Tomorrow morning when the teacher asked, up would go her hand, but there they'd all sit stupid and with their mouths full of teeth. It did not seem much of a threat. The excited voices of the boys came drifting back to her.

Lina fixed her eyes hard upon a distant hazy swirling far out above the sea, wanting it to be stork but knowing all the time it was just a sea gull. She wouldn't play with Eelka again for a week! Maybe ten days even, maybe three weeks! Even if in all that time Jella and the rest left Eelka out of every one of their games. She wouldn't bother with Eelka either. She just wouldn't bother!

She stared hard at the gull. It was still a gull; it wasn't a stork. Suppose a whole big flock of storks came flying up out of the sea. The boys, jumping ditches, wouldn't even see them. But Lina had to admit to herself it wouldn't make much difference if they saw the storks or not. The storks wouldn't stay in Shora, and the boys couldn't make them stay, so what was the difference? Lina sighed. It was hard being the only girl in Shora.

She took off one of her wooden shoes and sat staring moodily into it. She caught herself doing it. It was a lonely habit. She often sat staring into her shoe. It somehow made her feel better and seemed to help her to think better, but she didn't know why. She often wished she could wear her wooden shoes in the schoolroom instead of just socks. The wooden shoes had to be left out in the porch. Lina was sure it would help no end if she could pull off one of her shoes and stare and dream into it awhile—especially before doing an arithmetic problem. Lina sighed. You couldn't dream with arithmetic. With arithmetic you could only think. It made arithmetic sort of scary. Hard and scary and not very exciting.

Storks were exciting! 'Wonder why? Wonder why?' Lina said quite hard into her wooden shoe. The words came bouncing back at her out of the hard wooden shell. She whispered it into the shoe; the words came whispering back. She sat dreaming, staring into the shoe. And the sea gull was swirling and sailing far out at sea.

Still thinking and dreaming about storks, she got up in her nice hazy daze and wandered away from the dike, one shoe in her hand. She went slowly down the street, staring intently at the roofs of all the houses as if she'd never seen them before. The village street lay quiet and empty. Lina had it to herself all the way through the village to the little school. The school had the sharpest roof of all, Lina decided. All the roofs were sharp, but the school's was the sharpest.

A thin faraway shout and a shrill laugh came through to her. She turned. In the far, flat distance she could see the boys. Now big Jella, it must be Jella, went sailing high over a ditch. Hard behind him, first sprinting, then sailing high on their poles, came the other three boys. And then there came one more; it must be Eelka. But Eelka disappeared—he must have gone into the ditch. Now there was a lot of shouting and running. Lina caught herself waiting anxiously for Eelka to appear out of the ditch. Then she remembered that she wasn't going to play with Eelka for three weeks. She turned her back to the distant boys. 'I hope he went in up to his neck,' she heard herself saying half-aloud. It surprised her. For now it didn't matter whether or not Eelka went into the water up to his neck; it didn't matter that the boys were having fun. She knew why the storks didn't come to build their nests in Shora. The roofs were all too sharp! But not only did she know the reason why, she also knew what to do about it! They had to put a wagon wheel on top of one of the roofs—a wagon wheel just like her aunt in Nes had on her roof. Tomorrow morning she would spring it on them in the schoolroom. They'd be surprised!

Lina started to hurry back to the village, almost as if she had to hurry to tell someone. She put her wooden shoe back to hurry better. There wasn't anyone there, she knew. The boys were playing in the fields; the teacher had gone. She could go home and tell her mother, but she would tell her mother anyway. It just seemed to her there had to be somebody *new* to tell it to—she had that feeling. There wasn't anyone like that. The whole street lay empty. It made her hurrying suddenly seem senseless. Lina slowed herself by staring at a house.

Once more Lina dawdled down the street, once more she stood a dreamy while before each house. Her shoe came off again. She was staring up at the roof of Grandmother Sibble III's house when the old lady came out. It startled Lina.

'I know I'm a nosy old creature,' Grandmother Sibble III said, 'but there you stand again, staring.

I've been watching you wandering from the dike to the school and back again like a little lost sheep.'

Lina laughed a polite little laugh. 'Oh, I'm not exactly wandering. I'm wondering.'

'Oh,' said the old lady, mystified. 'Well, I suppose wondering is always better than wandering. It makes more sense.' She chuckled a nice little old lady's chuckle.

They looked at each other. And Lina thought how she had never talked much to Grandmother Sibble III except to say a polite 'hello' as she walked by. Now she did not know just what to say to her.

The old lady was still looking at her curiously. 'Is that why you have your shoe in your hand?' she said gently. 'Because you were wondering so hard?'

In surprise Lina glanced down at her hand holding the wooden shoe. She reddened a little and hastily slipped it on her foot. What must Grandmother Sibble think—not that she was her grandmother, she was just the grandmother of the whole village, the oldest old lady. It certainly must have looked silly, her hobbling down the street on one shoe, carrying the other. No wonder Grandmother Sibble III had come out of the house!

'I . . .' Lina said, trying to explain. She giggled a little. 'Oh, isn't it silly?' She fished in her mind for some sensible explanation None would come. But Grandmother Sibble III wasn't standing there grinning in a superior, adult way. She just looked—well, mystified and inquisitive. Lina decided to tell her. 'It does look silly and odd, but it somehow helps me think better to look into my shoe. Then when I get to thinking really hard, I forget to put it back on again,' she said defensively.

'Why, yes,' the old lady said immediately. 'Isn't it funny how odd little things like that help? Now I can think much better by sort of rocking myself and sucking a piece of candy, and I've done it ever since I was a little girl like you.' She carefully settled herself on the top step of her brick porch. She looked as if she was settling herself for a good, long chat. 'Now of course, I've just got to know what it was you were thinking about so hard it made you forget your shoe.' She chuckled her little old chuckle again. 'And if you don't tell me, I won't sleep all night from trying to guess.'

They laughed together. Grandmother Sibble patted the spot next to her. 'Why don't you come and sit down with me and tell me about it.'

Lina eagerly sat down—close, exactly where the old lady had patted. Old Grandmother Sibble was nice, she thought to herself. It was a nice surprise. She didn't talk to you as if you were a tiny tot, almost a baby, and miles of years away, the way grown-ups usually did. She even understood silly girl things like looking into a wooden shoe. She understood it the way a girl friend—if you had a girl friend—would understand. A girl friend who also had silly tricks and secretly told you about them. Aloud Lina said, 'I was thinking about storks, Grandmother Sibble. Why storks don't come and build their nests in Shora.'

Grandmother Sibble looked thoughtful. 'Well, that is a thing to ponder all right. No wonder you had your shoe off. We here in Shora are always without storks.'

'But I worked out why,' Lina told the old lady proudly. 'Our roofs are too sharp!'

'Well, yes . . . Yes, I suppose so,' the old lady said carefully, sensing Lina's sharp excitement. 'But that could be remedied by putting a wagon wheel on the roof, couldn't it? The way they do in the other villages?'

'Yes, I'd thought of that,' Lina said promptly. 'My aunt in Nes has a wagon wheel on her roof, and storks nest on it every year.'

'Ah, yes,' the old lady said, 'but doesn't your aunt's house have trees around it, too?'

'Yes, it has,' Lina said, looking in surprise at the little old lady. Why, Grandmother Sibble must have been thinking about storks, too. It seemed amazing, the old, old lady thinking about storks. 'I'm afraid I never thought about trees. Well, just because there are no trees in Shora—so I didn't think about trees.' Lina's voice faded away. Here was a whole new thing to think about.

'Would a stork think about trees?' the old lady wanted to know. 'It seems to me a stork would think about trees. And it seems to me that in order to figure out what a stork would want, we should try to think the way a stork would think.'

Lina sat bolt upright. What a wonderful thing to

14

say! Lina fumbled for her shoe while she eagerly looked at the old lady.

'You see, if I were a stork, even if I had my nest on a roof, I think I would still like to hide myself in a tree now and then and settle down in the shade and rest my long legs. Not be on the bare peak of a roof for everybody to see me all the time.'

Lina pulled her feet up under her and looked down confusedly at her wooden shoes. She really needed her wooden shoe now. Her thoughts were racing.

'You see, years ago,' Grandmother Sibble was explaining, 'oh, years and years ago when I was the only girl in Shora, the way you are the only girl now, there were trees in Shora and there were storks! The only trees in Shora grew on my grandmother's place. My grandmother was then the only grandmother of Shora. She was Grandmother Sibble I, just like I am now Grandmother Sibble III and you would someday be Grandmother Sibble IV if your mother had named you Sibble instead of Lina. I asked her to! Oh, I had no business asking—we're not even related—but it just seems there should always be a Grandmother Sibble in Shora. But that's beside the point.

'The point is, my grandmother's little house stood exactly where your school stands now but, oh, so different from your little naked school. Really different! My grandmother's house was roofed with reeds and storks like reeds. And my grandmother's house was hidden in trees. And storks like trees. Weeping willow trees grew around the edge of a deep moat that went all around my grandmother's house. And in the shadowy water under the hanging willows, pickerel swam in the moat. And over the moat there was a little footbridge leading right to my grandmother's door. And in one of the willows there was always a stork's nest, and there was another nest on the low reed roof of my grandmother's house. As a little girl I used to

15

stand on the footbridge and think that I could almost reach up to the low roof of the little house and touch the storks, so close they seemed.'

'Oh, I didn't know. I never knew,' Lina said breathlessly.

Grandmother Sibble did not seem to hear. Her eyes were looking far, far back. She shook her head. 'A storm came,' she said. 'As storms so often come to Shora. But this was a real storm. The wind and waves roared up the dike for longer than a week. For a whole week the water pounded and the salt spray flew. The air was full of salt; you even tasted the salt on your bread in your houses. And when it was all done, there were only three willows left at Sibble's Corner—that is what they called my grandmother's house, because everybody gathered there of a warm summer day to sit and chat and rest from work in the only shade in Shora, to talk and to lean their tired backs against the only trees. Then even those three left-over trees sickened and died. Their leaves had just taken in too much salt that long week of the storm.

'Later, after Grandmother Sibble I died, they came and tore down her house and chopped out the old rotted stumps of the willows and filled the moat with earth. Then there was nothing for years and years, until they built your naked little school on the same spot. But the storks never came back.'

Lina sat wide-eyed, hugging her knees, staring straight ahead, drinking it in, dreaming it over—the things the old lady had said—dreaming the picture. It sounded like a faraway tale, and yet it had been! Grandmother Sibble III had seen it! She had thought as a little girl that she could reach up and touch the storks, it had been so real and so close. Right in Shora!

'I never knew. I never knew,' Lina whispered to herself. 'And even a little footbridge,' she told herself and hugged her knees.

16

Grandmother Sibble III roused herself. 'So you see you mustn't think our sharp roofs is the whole story, must you?' she said softly. 'We must think about other things, too. Like our lack of trees, our storms, our salt spray. We must think about everything. And to think it right, we must try to think the way a stork would think!'

Grandmother Sibble said 'we'!

'Then have you been thinking about storks, too?' Lina asked in astonishment.

'Ever since I was a little girl. And ever since then I've wanted them back. They're lucky and cosy and friendly and, well, just right. It's never seemed right again—the village without storks. But nobody ever did anything about it.'

'Teacher says,' Lina told the old lady softly, 'that maybe if we wonder and wonder, then things will begin to happen.'

'Is that what he said? Ah, but that is so right,' the old lady said. 'But now you run into the house. There's a little tin on my kitchen shelf and in it there are wineballs. You get us each a wineball out of the tin. Then I'll sit in my porch and you sit in yours, and we'll think about storks. But we'll think better each in his own porch, because often thinking gets lost in talking. And maybe your teacher is right—that if we begin to think and wonder, somebody will begin to make things happen. But you go and find the tin; I can think much better sucking a wineball. And you take one, too. You watch if it doesn't work much better than looking inside an old wooden shoe.'

Lina had never been in Grandmother Sibble III's house before, never in the neat kitchen. There was the shelf, and there was the candy tin. There were storks on the candy tin! Pictures of storks in high sweeping trees were all around the four sides of the candy tin. On the lid was a village, and on every house there was a huge, ramshackle stork nest. In every nest tall storks stood as though making happy noises with their bills up into a happy blue sky.

Lina kept turning the candy tin to see the pictures again and again. Suddenly she woke up to the fact that she was staying in Grandmother Sibble's house a long, long time. Her first time in Grandmother Sibble's house, too! What would she think? She hastily shoved the candy tin back on its shelf and hurried to the porch.

'Grandmother Sibble, storks on your candy tin! And on every roof a nest! Oh . . .' Suddenly Lina realized she'd forgotten the wineballs. She raced back. It was hard not to look at the storks, but she kept her face partly turned away and picked out two round, red wineballs. Then she ran back. 'I forgot all about the wineballs,' she apologized.

'Yes, I know,' Grandmother Sibble said gently, for she saw that Lina—though looking straight at her while handing her her wineball—was not seeing her at all. Lina had dreams in her eyes. Lina was seeing storks on every roof in Shora. The old lady quietly let Lina wander off the porch and to her own house. Lina had dreams in her eyes and would not hear words anyway.

In her own porch Lina looked back for the first time. There sat Grandmother Sibble III rocking herself a little and sucking her wineball. But the dream Lina was dreaming was not just about storks—not directly. Later she would think about storks, try to think the way a stork would think, as Grandmother Sibble had said. But now she thought about Grandmother Sibble, who had a candy tin in her house with storks on it and who had known storks and who, when she was a little girl, had imagined she could reach up and almost touch the storks.

But that was not the wonder either, not quite. The

18

real wonder was that, just as the teacher had said, things *had* begun to happen. Begin to wonder why, the teacher had said, and maybe things will begin to happen. And they had! For there sat Grandmother Sibble III in the porch of her little house, and suddenly she had become important. She wasn't just an old person any more, miles of years away, she was a friend. A friend, like another girl, who also wondered about storks.

Lina looked again at the little old lady, sitting there in the porch. She marvelled; she sat feeling nice and warm about a little old lady who had become a friend. It was a lovely feeling, as sweet as a wineball, as sweet as a dream. Lina took one shoe off and peered into it. Why, storks did bring good luck! The storks had made a friend for her. Why, now when the boys left her out of their games, she could go to Grandmother Sibble, and they would sit and talk and chat. Lina looked up out of the shoe triumphantly. Why, yes!

CHAPTER III

Wagon Wheel

IN THE morning it was school again. There they were in the schoolroom again, the five boys and Lina and the teacher. But this Saturday morning they did not start out by singing the old, old song about their country— 'my lovely spot of ground, my fatherland, where once my cradle stood'. No, they sat quietly as the teacher stood looking at each one of them in turn. And then he said, 'Who wondered why? And where did it lead you?'

Lina's hand shot up. To her amazement every hand shot up with hers, even Jella's and Eelka's. The teacher looked so happy and pleased about it, it made Lina furious. 'Why, Teacher, they never did! They went ditch jumping.'

She clapped her hand to her mouth, but it was too late. She wasn't a telltale. It was just that it had come boiling up out of her, because it had made her so furious. They were fooling the teacher, and it was making him happy.

The teacher looked at her a short moment. He seemed surprised. He turned away from her to Jella. Jella sat there in the front seat, big and stubborn and angry. He was really angry with her. But the teacher was saying, 'Well, Jella, and what did you think was the reason why storks do not come to Shora?'

20

'Oh, I didn't think,' Jella told the teacher honestly. 'I asked my mother.'

The teacher smiled. 'Well, next to thinking, asking is the way to become wise. What did your mother say?'

'She said storks don't come to Shora because they never did. She said storks go back every year to the same nesting spots. So if they never came to Shora, they never will. So there's just nothing to be done about it, she said.'

Lina sat in her seat, trembling with eagerness to tell them that storks had once come to Shora, to tell them what Grandmother Sibble had said. She wanted to wave her hand frantically. But all the boys were angry with her, and even the teacher had been surprised and disappointed. It was a woebegone feeling, but still she had to do something. She quivered with eagerness. Then she *was* waving her hand, almost getting up out of her seat, but the teacher didn't take notice. She had to tell them! Lina heard herself saying out loud, 'Oh, but storks did once upon a time come to Shora!'

They all turned to her, even the teacher. The next moment Lina was excitedly telling the room the story that Grandmother Sibble had told her about Sibble's Corner and the storks and the willow trees all around and the moat with the footbridge. About storks right here in the exact spot where the school now stood! She even told about the pickerel in the moat.

Jella in the front seat turned right around when he heard about the pickerel. He forgot he was angry with her; he forgot he was in school. He just said right out loud, without permission, 'Oh, boy, pickerel! Were they big, Lina?'

All the boys had big excited eyes. They seemed to be much more interested in the pickerel than in the storks. All but Eelka. Eelka raised his hand, and now he was saying in his slow way, 'What Lina said about trees. You know, Teacher, that is exactly what I thought when I wondered why. Storks don't come to Shora because we have no trees!'

Eelka's desk was next to Lina's. She twisted in her seat to stare at him. How did he dare? He'd wondered why! He'd gone jumping ditches!

It was as if Eelka knew what she was thinking, for he calmly told the teacher, 'I don't suppose I would have thought of trees. It was really when I jumped right smack into the middle of a ditch and went under that I thought of it. I really got soaked, and I wished there was a tree to hang my clothes on. But there aren't any trees, so I had to go home dripping wet. Boy, did I catch it from my mother!'

The teacher laughed as long and hard as the class. Even Lina had to laugh.

'Well, Eelka,' the teacher said, 'even though you had to do your thinking under water, it was still good thinking.' His eyes were bright with laughter as he turned to the class. 'All right, now. Does everyone agree with Eelka that the number one reason why storks do not come to Shora is because we have no trees?' He turned to the blackboard and wrote in big letters:

THE REASONS WHY STORKS DO NOT COME TO SHORA

Under the words he put a big number one and waited.

'I still think the number one reason is what my mother said,' Jella spoke up.

'Ah, but Lina has just told us that storks used to come to Shora. In fact, Jella, Grandmother Sibble III has seen storks nesting above the spot where you are sitting now. Where our school now stands. Imagine it!' said the teacher.

'I think maybe my mother was wrong,' Jella said slowly. He seemed to hate to have to admit it. He looked up at the ceiling in a troubled way.

Then Auka raised his hand and quietly said, 'Then the number one reason is still NO TREES.'

'That's what Grandmother Sibble thinks, too,' Lina told the class honestly. 'She says storks like shelter and trees and hiding and a shady place to rest their long legs. She said she would if she were a stork! And Grandmother Sibble told me the way to find out what a stork would want is to try and think like a stork.'

The teacher stood looking at Lina. 'Is that what Grandmother Sibble III told you? I think that is wonderful,' he said. He turned back to the class. 'Well, are we agreed then that the number one reason for no storks in Shora is no trees?' He turned toward the board with his chalk as if to write it down.

Lina frantically waved her hand to stop him. 'Not trees—roofs!' she almost shouted when the teacher did not turn. 'Teacher,' she said desperately to the teacher's back, 'even though Grandmother Sibble and everybody thinks it is trees, it has to be roofs. Storks don't just build nests in trees, they build their nests on roofs, too. But our roofs in Shora are too sharp! Oh, it just has to be roofs,' she pleaded. 'Because we can put wheels on the roofs for storks to build their nests on, but we can't do anything about trees.' Breathlessly she told the class about Grandmother Sibble's candy tin with the picture of a whole village on its lid and stork's nests on every roof—because there was a wheel on every roof for the storks to build their nests on!

Pier and Dirk said almost together, 'Oh, man, imagine a nest on every roof in Shora!'

'Even on the roof of our school!' Auka shouted.

'But that's just it. That's just it!' Lina all but shouted at them. 'There's not a single wheel on any roof in Shora, because, just like Grandmother Sibble, everybody else must have thought it was no trees. So nobody ever put up a wheel. Nobody even tried! But how can we know if we don't try?'

Lina sat back waiting breathlessly, hopefully looking at the teacher. Oh, she had to be right! Teacher had to think it was right.

The teacher liked their excitement. He stood before the blackboard turning the piece of chalk in his hand in no hurry to write anything down. He looked at the boys who were still looking in surprise at Lina. He looked at Lina. 'Aha,' he said proudly. 'Little Lina.' And then he wrote on the blackboard Lina's reason in big white letters:

NO WHEELS ON OUR SHARP ROOFS

He turned back to the class. 'Could it be?' he asked. 'If we put wheels on our sharp roofs, could there be storks on every roof in Shora, the way Lina saw it in the picture on the candy tin?'

'Aw, that was just a picture,' Jella said scornfully. 'You can put anything in a picture. All that is a dream.'

'Ah, yes, that's all it is,' the teacher said. 'As yet! But there's where things have to start—with a dream. Of course, if you just go on dreaming, then it stays a dream and becomes stale and dead. But first to dream and then to do—isn't that the way to make a dream come true? Now sit for a moment, picture it for a moment: our Shora with trees and storks. Now Shora is bare, but try to see Shora with trees and storks and life. The blue sky above and the blue sea stretching behind the dike and storks flying over Shora. Do you see it?'

'Trees won't grow in Shora,' Jella argued stubbornly. 'It's the salt spray and the wind and storms. There's only one tree in Shora, and that's a small

24

cherry tree in the back yard of legless Janus. But the yard's got a high wall around it, so high you can hardly climb it. The cherry tree grows against the sunny wall of the house, and Janus pets it and guards it. He won't let a bird or a kid get even one cherry. Not one!'

'Well, but doesn't that show us something?' the teacher said. 'That to raise trees in Shora we must perhaps protect them. And couldn't we raise trees that could withstand the storms and salt spray—stouter and stronger than willows? There must be trees that grow along the sea. Or maybe we would have to protect the willows with a windbreak of poplar trees. The point is, if trees once grew here, couldn't we make them do it again?'

'Oh, but that would take too long,' Dirk said. 'That would take years.'

'Making dreams become real often takes long,' the teacher said. 'I don't mean that it should be done at once. Our first problem is how to make just one pair of storks come to nest in Shora. That is what we are trying to do now, by first thinking out the reasons why the storks don't nest in Shora. But after that . . . If trees once grew where our school now stands, wouldn't they grow there again? Think of it. Trees all around our school!'

'And a moat with pickerel in it,' Jella promptly added. 'We boys could even dig it ourselves, and Lina could make hot chocolate milk for the diggers.'

'Yes, Jella, now you are getting into the spirit of it. For that matter, we could even plant our own little trees. But first, before we can even start to think of all that, what must we do?'

'Find a wheel to put on a roof,' Lina promptly cried.

'Ah, hah,' the teacher said. 'Now we are getting to something that we can do. Now do you see? We wondered why and we reasoned it out. Now we must do. Now we must find a wagon wheel, and then we must put it up on a roof. But behind doing that lies the long dream—storks on every roof in Shora. Trees! Maybe even a moat around the school. Can you picture our Shora like that?'

Excitement was in his voice; excitement was in the whole room. Lina couldn't sit still. She squirmed and squirmed, and then her hand shot up. 'And a footbridge leading right to the door! We'd go over the footbridge to school. Teacher,' she pleaded, 'I could get Grandmother Sibble's candy tin. Then we could all see what Shora would be like with storks and trees.'

The teacher nodded. 'Run then, Lina.'

Grandmother Sibble III had no objections whatever to Lina's taking the candy tin to school. 'Oh, no, child, keep it there as long as you like. Keep it until you get real storks in Shora.' She opened the tin and took out a wineball. 'Why, enough left for a wineball for each of you.'

In the schoolroom they passed the candy tin around from hand to hand, and each one looked at all the pictures on the sides and on the lid. Each took out one wineball before reluctantly passing the tin on. The teacher took out the last wineball and then put the candy tin on the top ledge of the blackboard, on its side, so that the village with the trees and the storks on every roof could be seen from every point in the room. And underneath the tin, he wrote on the blackboard in big letters: 'COULD IT BE?'

He turned back to the class. 'Imagine a zebra in Shora,' he said. 'Imagine the long necks of two giraffes poking over the top of the dike. Imagine a giraffe running along our dike.'

'Imagine a lion in Shora!' Auka said.

'Yes, Auka, even imagine a lion in Shora,' the teacher surprisingly agreed. 'A good lion, a gentle lion in our street. But isn't it almost like that with storks? Do you know where our storks come from—where

26

they are when they aren't in Holland? Imagine the heart of Africa. The head of a big river deep in Africa, where it isn't a river any more but little rivulets and reedy swampland and marshes that go to make the beginnings of a big river. That's where our storks are now. Down there among the zebras and the herds of gazelles, among the lions and the buffaloes. Do you see our stork? There's an old rhinoceros right behind him, skulking in the brush. Do you see the stork standing on the banks of the river where the river begins? Just beyond him in the swampy river is a herd of hippopotamuses, snorting and blowing in the deeper water. And the stork lives among them! Until a time comes and the big noble bird spreads his great wings, flaps his big wings, and comes out of the wilds of Africa to live among us. A great wild bird, yet tame and gentle, living among us in a village. Isn't it wonderful? And maybe, just maybe—— It's still a dream. We haven't even a wheel as yet; we don't even know what roof we'll put it on.'

'Oh, yes, we do! Oh, yes, we do!' the whole class shouted. 'It's got to go right on the roof of our school.'

'Why, yes,' the teacher said. 'Why, of course! Then who's going to look for a wagon wheel? Look for a wagon wheel where one is and where one isn't; where one could be and where one couldn't possibly be?'

They were all too breathless to say a word. But Jella hastily swallowed his wineball whole, then blurted it out for all of them. 'We all are. From the moment school is over until we find one.'

The teacher nodded and nodded. 'That's how we'll begin to make a dream come true. We'll begin today. It's Saturday, and we have our free afternoon before us. We'll have a whole afternoon to try to find a wagon wheel. We'll really work at it, because that is how to start to make a dream come true. . . . But now let's turn to arithmetic.'

CHAPTER IV

Jella and
the Farmer

THEY had stumbled through arithmetic, they had been stupid about grammar, but when it came to penmanship—well, there just was no way to keep their minds on penmanship.

Lina was the first one to give up in despair. The teacher, walking along the aisle, had stopped to study her copybook. Lina promptly gave up. 'Teacher,' she said, 'I can't sit still, and when you can't sit still, you can't do penmanship. It's all jiggly.'

The whole class stopped. 'Let's make plans,' Auka suggested hopefully. 'We ought to make plans about how we're going to get a wheel for those two storks.'

'The storks will be coming awfully soon, won't they?' Eelka asked the teacher.

'Well, the stork season is here; there's no evading

28

that,' the teacher said slowly. 'And since you've brought it up so shrewdly, Eelka, I can't deny that we haven't much time.'

'Then why are we wasting it on penmanship?' Jella said. He held up his copybook for the teacher and all to see. He had done about three words of penmanship, but then he'd given up and drawn a picture of a big stork with a big fish held crosswise in its bill. 'That fish is a pickerel out of our own moat,' Jella explained.

The teacher laughed. 'You're not only thinking far ahead, you're drawing far ahead, Jella; and it isn't penmanship. But if you're all going to write in your copybooks like quavery old men—Grandmother Sibble III could write a steadier hand than you, Lina —well . . .'

The teacher paused; the whole class waited expectantly. 'Now listen, boys and Lina, yesterday we lost an hour, and if now I dismiss school again a whole hour early . . . How much does it mean to you? Would you be willing to come to school—after this is all over —a whole free Saturday afternoon to make up for this lost time?'

'Oh, yes,' they all said together. 'Oh, sure.'

'Then it's agreed,' the teacher said promptly. 'Now we've an hour before noon. Suppose we spend that hour looking through Shora. In the afternoon we'll branch out over the countryside. We'll go to every farm down every road.'

'Oh, boy,' Auka said, 'if we each found a wheel, we'd have a wheel for almost every house in Shora.'

'We've got to find one for Grandmother Sibble's house, too,' Lina reminded all of them.

'Everybody but legless Janus,' Jella immediately agreed. 'All I'd give him is a crack on the head.'

'Not so fast, not so fast,' the teacher cautioned them. 'Our whole problem is to find one wheel. Don't start rolling your wheels to the school and up on every roof of Shora. Find just one. I'm afraid that'll be difficult enough. And remember when the clock in the tower strikes twelve, all report back to school. If we haven't found a wheel, I'll assign each one a road to search this afternoon.'

They streamed out of the school. It was exciting to rush out of school and down the village street, to scatter and branch out in a search of every yard and barn and shed.

They were tremendously hopeful at first, but the short last hour of Saturday morning rushed on. And now it hadn't seemed like an hour at all—hardly ten minutes—when the big clock in the tower was bonging out the hour of twelve. It bonged twelve slow times. All over the village every school child was counting the strokes. It was hard to believe the clock, but twelve o'clock it was. The clock had counted right.

In the attic of his own house, Jella counted the bongs of the clock. He looked disgustedly through the little dusty attic window up at the great white face of the clock. It *was* twelve; the big bronze hands said so, too. And here he sat empty-handed in the attic of his own house. He was muddy and wet. He'd been across back gardens and over ditches but had ended up empty-handed in his own dusty attic. It had seemed silly to think that there'd be a wagon wheel up in the attic, but the teacher had said to look where a wheel could be and where it couldn't possibly be. Well, a wheel couldn't possibly be in an attic, and it wasn't!

Jella had found a bow. In his own attic he'd found a bow that he'd never known about but no arrows. Now he sat behind the dusty window and twanged the empty bow at the offending round white face of the clock in the tower.

Jella glanced down from his high window into the back yard of Grandmother Sibble's house next door.

The cellar trap door flew open, and there came Auka struggling up out of the cellar with a big stone crock.

Auka set down the crock and stared up at the clock in the tower. Auka felt cheated and disappointed. He'd been through every shed in Shora, except the shed of legless Janus, of course. You didn't just go up to Janus and say, 'May I look through your shed?' You'd get your head knocked off!

Grandmother Sibble's house had been his last house. It had no shed. Auka had been desperate enough to ask Grandmother Sibble if he might look through her cellar.

'It's no use, Auka,' Grandmother Sibble had said. 'I know exactly what's in my old cellar—one crock of pickled cabbage. I don't keep things there any more; it's too difficult for me to get down there. But I can't stand the smell of pickled cabbage, so there it is.'

'The teacher told us,' Auka had said doubtfully, 'to look where a wheel could be and where it couldn't possibly be.'

'Well, you've come to the right place,' Grandmother Sibble had chuckled. 'A wheel couldn't possibly be in my cellar. But your teacher is right—that's the only way to find things. So go ahead and look, else you won't feel satisfied. And while you're there will you carry the cabbage out into the back yard for me? It's even beginning to smell through the floor.'

Now as he stood staring up at the tower clock with the crock at his feet, Auka's eye suddenly caught a movement behind the high attic window next door. Jella was aiming an arrowless bow at him. 'Look what I found!' Jella shouted through the window.

'That's not a wagon wheel,' Auka yelled back.

'No, but, boy, could you have fun with it if you had some arrows! What did you find?'

'A crock of pickled cabbage,' Auka yelled, and suddenly he grinned.

Jella made a face. 'What good is pickled cabbage for storks?'

Auka shrugged. 'About as much good as a bow, I guess. Come on, let's get back to school. It's twelve.'

In a barn at the edge of the village, Pier and Dirk heard the clock in the tower bong out the hour. It stopped them cold. They sat looking at each other guiltily. 'Twelve o'clock,' Dirk told Pier, 'and you and I just played.'

'Yeah, I know,' Pier said.

They had found a haymow in the barn. They had climbed to the top of the haymow. Of course, there had been no wagon wheel on top of the hay. They hadn't expected one. But as Pier had told Dirk virtuously, they were supposed to look where a wheel couldn't possibly be. Of course, having climbed to the top of the haymow, they'd had to slide down to the barn floor. That had been such fun they'd climbed right back, not even pretending to look for a wagon wheel now. It was amazing how fast an hour of fun had flown by. Now it was twelve. Pier looked at Dirk. Dirk looked at Pier. They sat in the hay that had slid down to the barn floor with them. Dirk looked at the sprawled hay and hastily jumped up. 'We haven't a wagon wheel,' he said woefully. 'All we've got is a mess.'

'Not even a spoke,' Pier said dolefully.

'Maybe we'd better grab up the hay and take it along,' Dirk suggested.

'Hay for a stork? It isn't a goat!'

'No, but we haven't got time to put it back on top of the mow. If we take it along and drop it somewhere, the farmer won't know we played in his hay.'

It seemed a good idea, at least it was about the best thing to do under the circumstances. They hastily scraped the sprawled hay together; each grabbed up an armful and started running toward school.

'Boy, that was fun,' Pier said. 'Wasn't it?'

'Yes,' Dirk said guiltily. 'But I hope somebody found a wheel.'

'Couldn't we take the hay to school and say it's for the storks to build a nest with?' Pier suggested. 'That would show we did something.'

'Maybe,' Dirk said doubtfully. 'But come on, run. It's way past twelve.'

When Dirk and Pier came running toward the schoolyard, Jella and Auka were already there with the teacher. Far behind Pier and Dirk came Eelka, pushing a high old perambulator. A distance behind Eelka, toward the canal end of the street, Lina came running empty-handed.

When they were all gathered in the schoolyard, the teacher looked at each one of them in turn. 'A bow, a baby carriage, two bundles of hay, but no wagon wheel,' the teacher said slowly. He looked at Auka. 'And what did you find, Auka?'

'A crock with pickled cabbage,' Auka said sombrely. 'But I didn't bring it here. I didn't think it would be any use to storks.'

'I didn't find anything at all,' Lina said hastily.

The teacher looked at the bundles of hay. 'Why did you bring hay?' he asked Pier.

'We thought if somebody had found a wheel,' Pier said vaguely, 'the hay might help the storks to start a nest.'

Dirk nodded. 'Yes, that's what we thought,' he said hastily.

'And you brought a perambulator, Eelka. Why?'

'I brought it for the wheels,' Eelka said. 'I suppose I didn't really think they were big enough. They were just the nearest thing to a wagon wheel that I could find. My mother let me have it,' he explained. 'She said since I was her last baby—definitely. And me going on twelve!'

'Some baby!' Jella said. 'Hah!'

'Then we've got nothing,' Lina said softly.

They stood in an unhappy little circle in the school-yard. They were so disappointed they did not look at each other. Somehow they all seemed to stare at the silly perambulator. Pier and Dirk stood there with their foolish armloads of hay. Pier suddenly stepped up and shoved his hay into Eelka's perambulator. In obvious relief Dirk shoved his armload on top of Pier's. There stood the perambulator with hay sticking out of it in every direction. Then nobody was looking at the pram; all eyes turned up.

There above the dike, high in the sky—high, white, huge wings flapping—two storks appeared from over the sea. Over the tower the storks winged still higher, flew high, flew straight, didn't dip down for Shora, did not even pause or circle. Then they were two white

34

winging dots disappearing fast in the enormous blue sky. Soon they were gone.

Slowly all the eyes came down. All were staring at the baby carriage again. Eelka's face became red. He muttered something that nobody understood, grabbed the perambulator, and shoved it disgustedly into the far corner of the schoolyard.

'Now if we only had a goat,' Auka said, looking at a tuft of hay that had spilled out of the pram and over his wooden shoes. No one laughed, and Auka wasn't smiling. No one said a thing. They were so quiet they could hear Lina swallowing hard a couple of times. That was the trouble with being a girl, Lina thought, you wanted to cry at things like this. But boys just looked angry and stubborn and disgusted. Suddenly Lina didn't swallow any more, didn't want to cry any more; she was angry.

Jella said it for them all. 'Look!' he savagely told them all. 'We can't mess around with bows and baby's prams and play in hay and fool around any more.' He took his bow and slung it hard toward the corner with the pram in it. It somehow caught in the hay sticking out of the perambulator, but Jella did not bother to notice it. 'Look,' he said, 'with the storks here, we've got to hunt for just one wheel, and we've got to hunt hard.' Jella was angry with himself and everybody else.

'Jella is right,' the teacher said. 'And I'm glad you all realize it now. However, we didn't really expect to find a wheel in Shora. Those are only the first two storks we have seen, so we shouldn't get too disappointed. Nevertheless, from now on the storks will be coming by two's, and then they'll be winging over Shora in flocks, and there's so little we can do to attract a couple of them to Shora. All we can do is put up a wheel; the rest is up to the storks. But that little we should do promptly, after that we can play.'

35

'We'll really hunt,' they solemnly promised.

'Fine. Then we'll start in again right after lunch. There are five roads spreading out from Shora. You boys will each take a road. Lina will take the dike.'

'The dike?' Lina said.

'Yes. I know there isn't much chance of a wagon wheel's being on the dike, but from the dike you can see all the little side roads and lanes and the isolated farmhouses that lie between the roads that the boys are taking. You can cover those, while the boys search every house and barn along their roads.'

'How far do we go?' Eelka asked.

'As far as it takes to find a wheel,' Jella answered him, before the teacher could say anything.

'I'll be in the school all afternoon and into the evening if that's necessary,' the teacher said. 'So be sure to report to me when you finish your search. If somebody finds a wheel, I'll ring the school bell. When you hear it, come back to school. Now everybody home for lunch. But don't forget. I still say look everywhere, where a wheel could be and where it couldn't possibly be. In spite of your disappointment in Shora this morning, the unexpected still always comes up to surprise us.'

It sounded hopeful again, and no more storks had appeared from over the sea. They all broke away and ran home as hard as they could.

It was four o'clock on Saturday afternoon. There was not a sound in Shora. Except for three small children playing in the village square at the foot of the tower, there wasn't a child. The five boys and Lina were scattered over the countryside, looking for a wagon wheel. In the doorway of the school, the teacher looked down the empty road that stretched from the school into the flat country. This was the road along which Jella was searching for a wagon wheel. The road lay deserted. Jella was nowhere in sight.

The teacher smiled a little to himself. 'Jella 's really got his heart in it now,' he softly told himself, 'and when Jella gets his heart into things, he's liable to hunt for a wheel into the next province.' From over the school, high in the sky, two storks appeared. They winged away in rapid, flapping flight. The teacher stood looking after them. The children in the country-side would see those storks, too. 'Just so they don't lose courage,' the teacher told himself.

When the teacher looked down the road again, it wasn't empty any more. Far away a wheel came rolling down the narrow country road. A boy was rolling it. He struggled it into an upright position whenever it fell and rolled it on. That must be Jella—only Jella was big and strong enough to wrestle a heavy wagon wheel down a road all by himself. Jella had a wheel! The teacher half turned as if to hurry into the school to ring the bell. 'Better wait,' he told himself. 'You can't tell what Jella may do when he has his heart set on things. No, better wait.'

He looked down the road again. Now no wheel was rolling down the road. Instead there was a farmer leading Jella to the school. The wheel was gone.

The teacher waited in the doorway of the school.

They came closer, the unwilling Jella and the big, angry farmer. The farmer was leading Jella down the road by the lobe of his ear. He had something red in his other hand. It looked like a piece of red roof tile. The teacher waited.

At last, after a long, painful march down the road, Jella was being guided by his ear across the school-yard. Jella looked stubborn and guilty and angry all at the same time. He stared defiantly at his teacher as he neared the doorway, even though he had to hold his head carefully tilted against any painful jerks on his

37

ear. The pinched ear lobe really must be throbbing now.

'I didn't steal it,' Jella said morosely as the farmer halted him before the teacher. 'He says I stole it, but I didn't. I yelled and called all over that farm. But there was nobody. And that wheel hadn't been used for ages. It was even sunk in the mud, because it stood under the drip of the shed. It took all I had to get it loose, so long it had been standing there, and now he says I stole it.'

The farmer grimly let Jella talk, now he faced the teacher. 'What goes on in this school of yours here anyway?' he demanded. 'Teaching children to steal things from people! There I was deepening a ditch at the back of my farm. I poke my head out while I rest my back a minute, and there I see a wheel rolling down the road. I look at my shed, and my wagon wheel isn't in its place against the shed wall. It's *my* wheel rolling down the road! So I run and run and jump ditches to catch up with this boy, and I still can't believe it. In broad daylight! When I stopped at the shed, sure enough my wheel was gone, and in its place all there was was this.' He shoved a broken piece of red roof tile at the teacher.

On the tile Jella had scratched with a nail: 'I'm taking the wagon wheel to put on the roof of our school for storks to build a nest on. We want storks to come to Shora again. I'll bring it back as soon as the storks have finished with it. Jella Sjaarda.'

The teacher forced himself not to smile. The hot-eyed farmer was watching him every moment while he read. 'Well,' the teacher said slowly, feeling his way, 'at least it isn't a downright thief who leaves a note and signs his name after he's taken something. And thieves hardly ever promise to return what they steal. So if we do teach them to steal at this school, you've got to admit we teach them to do it differently.' He

38

grinned good-naturedly at the man. 'You can see Jella meant to return it.'

'Sure, I've got to wait for my wheel until storks lay eggs and make nests, and after the storks have gone, I can use my own wheel again,' the farmer said hatefully. 'I need that wheel! I need my wagon only in spring and autumn, but when I need it, I need it. In fact, I'd planned to put the wheel back on the wagon this afternoon, and there it went rolling down the road.' The idea of his wheel rolling down the road made him furious all over again.

The farmer kept a wrathful hold on Jella's ear.

'If you would let go of his ear,' the teacher said, 'Jella won't run away, I promise you. I can maybe explain how Jella came to take the wheel without your permission. I'm not excusing it, understand—just explaining it—because you look like a man who would

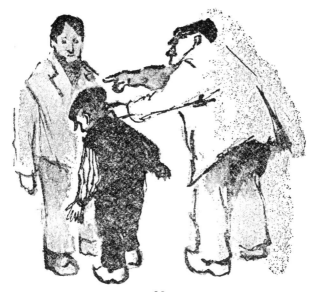

understand. You look to me as if you were once a boy just like Jella yourself—a boy who, once he sets his heart on something, stops at almost nothing. Didn't you as a boy sometimes take something when you couldn't get it any other way?'

The farmer relaxed a little. He almost started grinning, but he made it a scowl. 'Yes,' he said gruffly, 'because I wanted a bow and arrows. All the kids had bows and arrows, all but me. How I suffered, because I was the biggest of the whole lot. My mother wouldn't let me. She was afraid I'd somehow shoot myself, how I don't know. I didn't even have a knife—on account of my mother—to make myself a bow and arrows. And here I was the biggest kid—just as big and tough as this one.' He looked at Jella appraisingly. 'No, bigger. Well, I got the knife—don't ask me how—then I made the bow and arrows, and then I was happy. My grandfather caught me returning his knife. How he warmed my breeches! Well, he could have skinned me with the knife; I was still happy. I had my bow and arrows.'

'Well, there you see,' the teacher said. 'And now you've warmed Jella's ear. And Jella still doesn't have the wheel he wanted so badly.'

The man looked at the red, swollen ear.

The teacher explained the school's great project of luring just two storks back to Shora, and the man listened. He nodded understandingly when the teacher finished. 'I'll tell you,' he began, but then he looked at Jella's ear again. 'Better put a cold wet rag against that ear, kid,' he interrupted himself. 'Yes, I can understand now why he did it in all the excitement. But as I started to say, he can still have the wheel in about a week, as soon as I've finished with the wagon. He can have it till autumn. After this week I won't need the wagon again until autumn—not on my little farm.'

'That would be too late, wouldn't it?' Jella anxiously asked the teacher. 'I counted at least five pairs of storks flying over this afternoon. They're starting to come so fast, there can't be a stork left in Africa among those rhinoceroses you were telling us about. In Africa they live right among the lions and hippos and zebras,' he eagerly explained to the farmer. 'But here they live right in our villages with us.' Then he said unhappily, 'Except Shora, of course.'

'Yes, I'm afraid in a week it might be too late, Jella,' the teacher said. He turned to the farmer. 'Could Jella help you with your wagon work on your farm? It seems to me he owes you at least that for all the inconvenience he caused you. And if he could help, it shouldn't take a week before you can let the school have the wheel.'

'It's a deal,' the farmer said promptly. 'I'll fix the wheel on the wagon as soon as I get back, and Jella can come and help me Monday or even right now. It's up to him.'

Jella stood thoughtfully feeling his throbbing ear. 'Do you still know how to make arrows?' he carefully asked the farmer. 'I've got a bow but no arrows.'

'Oh, sure,' the man said. 'And there's plenty of alder bushes right along the ditch I was deepening at the back of my farm. If you want arrows, I'll show you how.' He patted his pocket. 'I've got a knife of my own now,' he said with a grin.

'I'll be there,' Jella promised happily. 'But maybe this afternoon I ought to look some more for a wagon wheel. The storks are coming over so fast.' He looked at the teacher for approval.

'Suit yourself,' the farmer said. He strode off.

Jella tenderly pulled at the lobe of his sore ear and looked meekly at the teacher. 'I didn't mean to steal it,' he explained. 'But there was no one to ask and there was the wheel . . .' His voice trailed off. 'I'd better look some more,' he said lamely and walked away.

41

'Look but don't take without asking,' the teacher called after him. 'Just pinch your ear, if you're tempted.'

They both laughed a little. Then Jella turned to go and the teacher went back into the school. As Jella crossed the playground, four storks flew high overhead. 'Now, they're coming by fours,' Jella called to the teacher. Then he noticed that he was alone. He stared up at the storks again. Suddenly he shook his fist at them. 'Do we have to knock you down to get you to stop in Shora?'

His eyes fell on Eelka's perambulator in the corner of the schoolyard. The bow lay in the hay. If storks wouldn't stop in Shora, maybe he could make them stop. Shoot them down with bow and arrow! That might be the way to do it. Not kill them, just bring them down. Stuff them in a coop until there was a wheel up on the school. Then they'd have storks in Shora!

He eyed the open door of the school. On tiptoe he stole across the playground to the corner where the perambulator was and grabbed his bow. He ducked through a hedge and by a roundabout way—out of sight of the school windows—set off across the fields toward the farm with the wheel and the alder bushes for arrows.

CHAPTER V

Pier and Dirk and the Cherry Tree

IT SEEMED that even two different roads couldn't separate Pier and Dirk. They dutifully started out on the separate roads the teacher had assigned them. Dirk had taken the main road to the south that led to the village of Ternaad. Pier had a little earth road that angled and curved its unhurried way south-west from Shora. There were but four farms along the little road. Pier visited each farm, but it was for nothing. Even farmers, it seemed, did not keep spare wagon wheels.

'All my wheels are under my wagon,' the last farmer told Pier, 'and that's where I need them. I can't think of anything much more useless than a wagon without wheels, except maybe a man without legs.'

That was the last farm. After that the little road went in a long lazy loop and suddenly ended up in the Ternaad road that Dirk had taken. Pier settled himself in the grass—he'd wait for Dirk. Dirk couldn't possibly be past this point, because there were a lot of houses and farms along the Ternaad road. Pier sat a long time in the quiet. He wondered idly if the

43

farmer, who had said that about men without legs being useless, had been thinking about legless Janus. 'Wonder if he knows Janus?' Pier thought out loud. It must be awful not to have even one leg. A shark had bitten off both of Janus's legs in one bite! That was when Janus had still been a fisherman, like the rest of the men of Shora. He'd been knocked overboard one day, and just like that a shark had come along and bitten off both of Janus's legs, boots and all. Pier made a wide-jawed biting motion with his teeth. He could hear his teeth snap in the silence. He felt along the edges of his teeth. Man, one bite, boots and all!

Now Janus just sat in a wheel chair in his house or yard, and he'd become surly—the surliest man in Shora. Pier suddenly leaned forward and made a cutting motion with the edge of his hand across his legs. He tried to imagine what it would be like to be without legs. It wouldn't be any fun at all. It would make him surly, too. Heh, that was a crazy thing to think about, sitting here all by himself. It was so quiet here! He stared at his legs; just thinking crazy things like that seemed to make his legs feel numb and dead. But maybe it was because he'd been sitting in one position too long.

He hastily changed and sat cross-legged, glad he could double his legs under him. Why, sitting that way made him look almost legless! In a scary sort of way, he was enjoying the numb feeling in his legs which he imagined had been cut off. He looked around him in the stillness. How was he going to get home—legless? He pictured himself crawling home along the winding road, his stumps of legs dragging on behind. He moaned. He hastily tried to make it a little laugh, but it sounded like a groan in the deep country silence. 'Hey, cut it out!' he told himself.

That was the trouble with him when he was all alone without Dirk. He always thought up scary, silly,

44

hopeless things. He pulled his legs from under him. One leg prickled with little needle stabs all the way up! He poked the leg with his finger, jabbed all along it to see if it felt dead all over. He was so engrossed in his lonely little game he did not see Dirk come stealing toward him through the grass at the edge of the road. Suddenly Dirk's shadow fell across Pier's legs. Pier, startled, jerked his head up and glared at Dirk.

'I suppose that's hunting for a wagon wheel?' Dirk said.

'Well, I don't see you carting any wheels around,' Pier told his brother coldly. Dirk had scared him so!

'No, but at least I'm looking, not sitting in the grass.'

Pier caught himself saying, 'Well, you wouldn't look very far either if you had no legs.'

'Huh?' Dirk said.

Pier hastily changed the subject. 'Well, I finished my road. This is your road. So you just go on and finish yours. I'll wait here for you.'

'Well, I like that!' Dirk exploded. 'Wait here. Do you realize that this road goes all the way to Ternaad?'

'Well, maybe they've got some nice wheels in Ternaad.' Pier was paying Dirk back for scaring him, but he was secretly relieved Dirk was there. When he was with Dirk, he never got crazy, silly notions like having no legs. He certainly had no intention of sitting here alone again, waiting for Dirk. He jumped up. 'I'll go with you, Dirk.'

The next moment he crumpled to the ground. 'Dirk, my legs,' he gasped. 'My legs won't hold me!'

'They've gone to sleep because you've been sitting on them all afternoon,' Dirk said impatiently.

'Oh, yes, that's it,' Pier said in relief. Oh, but that had scared him for a moment! 'You know,' he told Dirk, 'for a moment there I thought I hadn't got any legs.'

'You've plenty of legs,' Dirk said. 'Just no sense.'

'Oh, is that so?' Pier said hotly. But then he grinned. 'Man, Dirk, I'm glad you came along. I don't like to go down roads and do things alone.'

'I don't either,' Dirk said. 'But come on, let's get going.'

'Right to Ternaad?' Pier asked. 'We won't get back till after dark, and I got hungry sitting here. I didn't eat much at lunch; I was too excited. Let's run home and ask Mum for something to eat.'

Dirk wavered. 'All right,' he agreed. 'I'm hungry, too. But we'll run all the way home and all the way back here. And then we'll go clear to Ternaad if we have to. And we won't fool around!'

Side by side they ran all the way back to Shora. In the village street they finally slowed to a panting walk. The street lay empty and quiet. There wasn't a sound anywhere; nothing stirred.

'Everybody's out in the country hunting,' Dirk said guiltily, 'but you had to go and get hungry.'

'You said you were hungry, too.'

'Yes, but not until you reminded me of it.'

Suddenly the silence in the village was shattered. There was a terrific banging and rattling and clatter of metal. The noise stopped. There was a moment's quiet. Then there came a savage, smashing sound. Dirk and Pier looked at each other and grinned. 'He missed,' Dirk said with satisfaction. 'Boy, did you hear that stone hit the fence? If that had hit a bird, there wouldn't be a feather left.'

'Wow!' Pier said.

They stood in the street, listening and grinning, waiting for more. They knew only too well what was happening. It was Janus. The cherries on Janus's tree must be beginning to ripen, and the birds were raiding it. But, as in every other spring, Janus was under the tree, protecting his cherries. Jana, Janus's wife, had

46

to climb up in the cherry tree every spring to hang a long rope, with pieces of tin strung on it, from the highest bough that would hold her weight. Janus couldn't do that—he had no legs. From the first day the cherries began to turn, Janus sat in his wheel chair under the tree to yank the rope and rattle the tin whenever a bird came near. The rattling tin took care of most birds but not of the magpies. Magpies were bold enough and clever enough to raid the tree and steal a cherry in spite of all the rattling and banging and clatter. For magpies and boys, Janus had other measures.

A little pile of stones always lay, ready for the grabbing, beside the wheel chair. That was for magpies and boys. Janus had a high board fence around his little yard. The top of this fence was studded with nails and sharp, jagged, broken necks of bottles. But in spite of nails and glass, the cherry tree was a terrible temptation to the boys in bare Shora. Janus's cherry tree was the only fruit tree in Shora and in the whole sea country around. In Shora a boy or a bird seldom got fruit. That's why Janus lived under his tree in the springtime.

Janus started to stand guard long before the cherries were ripe, for even a green cherry was a temptation to birds and boys—a green cherry being better than no cherry. But if the fence with its broken glass and nails failed to keep the boys out, there was the pile of stones gathered for Janus by his wife. On the way home from peddling her bread in the countryside, Jana had to fill the bottom of her breadbasket with stones gathered along the gravel roads. Every evening she supplied Janus with another day's ammunition. And Janus did not hesitate to hurl a stone at a boy trying painfully to worm himself over the fence without cutting himself and tearing his clothes. At boy or bird, Janus let fly, and through the years his aim had become deadly.

Even big Jella had failed, as often as he'd tried. If Jella couldn't manage it, who could? Jella often told how once he had got over the fence with only one long rip in his breeches. He'd dropped down inside Janus's yard and for once hadn't been noticed; Janus had been asleep under the cherry tree. On tiptoe Jella had gone toward the cherry tree and Janus. But just then a miserable magpie had screeched in the tree, and all in one moment it seemed—even before the screech was out of the silly bird's mouth—Janus had been wide-awake. For a moment Janus and Jella had stared at each other, then Jella had turned and raced for the back fence. He'd wildly thrown himself up against it, so scared he'd been. And Janus in the wheel chair had silently chased him. 'You wouldn't believe it,' Jella said every time he told about it, 'but him without legs, chasing me in a wheel chair in that boarded-up yard and never saying a word—I just stood up against that fence and let him grab me. I was paralysed.'

What had happened then? Even now, after a year, Jella didn't want to talk much about it. But it seemed Janus had taken Jella and flung him over his legless stumps, and then he had gone to work. All Jella would really say was, 'I wasn't scared paralysed any more when he got through with me—I just couldn't walk. That man's got the hardest hands. And he never said a word!'

Jella had never tried again.

Back in the fenced-in yard the tin began rattling and clattering once more. 'Come on,' Dirk said, 'we've got to get going.'

But Pier stood staring at the high fence behind which Janus was sitting. He didn't seem to hear Dirk. He stared. He stood in a half stoop, absent-mindedly rubbing his hand along his leg, and stared. 'Do you know what, Dirk?' he said suddenly. 'Teacher said to look everywhere, didn't he? Well, one thing's sure—nobody looked in Janus's yard. Suppose Janus had a wheel? Nobody knows what's in that yard. Just suppose there was a wheel there.'

'How would you get it if there was? How would you even get in his yard to look?' Dirk said, but he was interested now and stood looking from his scheming brother to the high fence. 'If Jella couldn't do it, how do you think you're going to do it?'

'Yes, but Jella was alone. We're two; we'd do it together.'

'How?'

'Well, you'd have to climb the fence right at the back.'

'And get my head knocked off with a stone?' Dirk said. 'Oh, thanks!'

'No, you wouldn't climb over the fence. You'd make a lot of noise *as if* climbing the fence, but you wouldn't get your head above it. See? Then when Janus heard you, he'd most likely wheel himself to the back fence and wait for you to come over so he could sock you with a stone. But if you make a lot of noise and keep climbing as if you can't quite make it, Janus won't hear me open the gate to his back yard. Then I can quickly sneak in and take a look around. And even grab a few cherries maybe. See? He won't be near his pile of stones. He'll be waiting for you at the fence. And if he does turn and see me, I'll just run out of the gate.'

'You'll run, if you don't get paralysed like Jella.'

'I won't get paralysed! Because sitting there in the country waiting for you, I kind of imagined how it feels without legs and how it must make you feel and everything and . . .' Pier gave up trying to explain; he didn't have the right words for it. It was impossible to explain even to Dirk.

Dirk was looking at him. 'Well, that is a plan,' he

grudgingly admitted. 'Well, if you dare, I dare.' Then Dirk started for the back fence.

Pier took his wooden shoes off. Shoes in hand he tiptoed behind Dirk as far as the high gate in the tall wooden fence. He crouched there, waiting for his brother to start making his climbing sounds. He tried to peer through a crack, but he could see nothing moving in the yard. Now he heard Dirk. Dirk was kicking his wooden shoes against the fence, making scraping sounds as if sliding down again after climbing up. Pier held his ear against the gate, listening for sounds that would tell him whether or not Janus was rolling his wheel chair to the back fence. Then at last he heard the slight squeak of the wheel chair. There was no other sound inside the yard. Janus himself was keeping deathly quiet. Now Dirk was making the clambering noises again, as if once more he was trying to climb up the board fence. The squeak of the wheel chair was fading away toward the back of the yard.

Pier jumped up, unlatched the gate, and softly pushed it open. To his relief the hinges did not squeal. To guard against it, he opened the gate no farther than he needed to squeeze through. He had his wooden shoes in one hand.

Pier was in the fenced-in yard. The scheme had worked! There lay the little pile of stones near the cherry tree, but Janus was far away from it. He was at the back fence, staring up, waiting for Dirk to come over. Pier flashed a curious look around. The tree was hanging full of glittering tin and full of green cherries. The end of the rope dangled under the tree. There was a small shed in one corner of the yard, but there was no wheel unless it was in the shed. On tiptoe in his stockinged feet, Pier stole toward the cherry tree.

As he silently crept under the cherry tree, Pier kept his eyes on Janus's motionless back. Then his heart stopped! Dirk was really noisy now. He'd thrown one hand over the top of the fence, so he could really make the climbing, kicking noises. Pier could see his fingers feeling and groping between the nails and bottlenecks for a better hold. And Janus sat looking up at the groping hand! Dirk mustn't! What was the matter with him?

Now Janus drew his arm back, his hand came back. He had a stone in his hand! He'd taken a stone with him! He was aiming for Dirk's hand. He'd smash Dirk's hand!

'Dirk, drop!' Pier yelled.

All in the single moment of the yell, the hand disappeared and Janus whirled in his wheel chair so fast it was unbelievable. Pier stood under the cherry tree, clutching his wooden shoes to him in nerveless hands. He wasn't going to be paralysed! He jerked his eyes away from Janus and sprinted for the gate.

'Stop, you. Stand right there, or *you* get the stone,' Janus shouted hoarsely. Janus still had the stone!

Slowly Pier turned to face Janus. It was awful to stand there helpless, waiting for the legless man to come and get him. Pier's eyes wavered toward the gate. The gate had fallen shut.

'Don't even try it,' Janus said coldly. 'That gate is fixed so that you can't open it from inside. That's a little trap I fixed up, so if a kid got in, he wouldn't get out without me putting my mark on him.'

Pier swallowed but did not speak. He couldn't. He stood rooted, scared eyes fixed on Janus. Now Janus stopped the chair directly before him. 'So you two were going to be tricky, huh? One distract me, while the other robbed my cherries right behind my back. Clever, huh?'

'No,' Pier said desperately. He had to swallow again before he could croak out more words. 'No, Janus, we weren't . . .'

'Weren't what?' Janus demanded.

51

'Going to rob your cherry tree. Honest, Janus, honest. We were just looking for a wagon wheel. We hadn't even thought about your cherries.'

'So, you're tricky, aren't you? Not only think out a clever way of getting in my yard, but you came sneaking in for wagon wheels, not for cherries. Oh, no, not for cherries.' Janus laughed a hoarse, mirthless laugh. 'Wagon wheels!'

Janus talked as if he were amused. But he wasn't amused, and that laugh wasn't a laugh, it was a threat. It was scarier than if Janus had ranted and raved and cursed. Now Janus leaned forward and looked hard at Pier. 'You are one of the twins, aren't you? You two do everything together, don't you? Well, all right, fine, then you've got to get what's coming to you together, too. Call your brother!'

'No!' Pier said desperately.

'Don't say "no" to me. Call him!' Janus's big arm flashed out. He grabbed Pier in one powerful motion and with just one arm twisted and spun Pier and threw him over his lap. There lay Pier across the stumps of legs. 'Call your brother!'

'No!' Pier yelled stubbornly, but it was half a scream.

'Wait, Janus, I'm coming,' Dirk yelled from behind the gate. He must have been crouched behind the gate, listening. The gate opened. Dirk came into the yard. The gate fell shut behind him.

Dirk stood before the wheel chair but carefully stayed out of reach of Janus. Pier twisted his head to look up at Dirk. They looked desperately at each other. 'Honest, Janus, we really didn't do it for cherries,' Dirk pleaded. 'Honest! Honest, we were looking for a wheel, just like Pier said. Oh,' he added then, 'I suppose we would have grabbed a few cherries while we were at it, but we came for a wagon wheel. It's for storks,' he explained.

'Talk some more. I like this,' Janus said. 'You're as clever as your brother.'

Dirk talked. Talked earnestly. 'We want to make storks come back to Shora again. We want to put a wagon wheel up on our school, and we've hunted everywhere. Then we got to thinking. Nobody would have dared to look in your yard, and then if you had a wheel . . .' Dirk talked desperately, talking and talking to postpone Pier's punishment, and Janus sat listening.

Dirk started all over again. He explained the whole project. He told Janus about the storks in Africa among lions and rhinoceroses and hippopotamuses. Dirk got the words all twisted. And then he ran out; he had no more to say. 'Just think,' he repeated helplessly, 'in Africa they live among wild beasts, but here they live right among people.'

'Well, now,' Janus said amazingly, 'if you ask me, living among people takes even more courage.' Suddenly he picked up Pier and set him down. 'Do you know,' he told Pier, 'I think I'm going to believe you two? Nobody could have cooked up a wild story like that about coming in here for a wheel and not for cherries, so it must be the truth. But now tell me— wouldn't you have grabbed a few handfuls of cherries while you were here?'

Dirk nodded timidly. 'I don't know how I could have just let them hang even if they are a little green.' he said slowly.

'Now there, that's better,' Janus told Pier. 'You've an honest brother. Any kid would, if he'd managed to get this far. But not you, oh, no, not you. You hadn't even thought about cherries!'

Pier got red in the face. He rubbed his leg awkwardly. 'Sure,' he said at last, 'but you had hold of me, not him. And maybe you didn't notice, but I had my wooden shoes in my hand.'

53

'So I wouldn't hear you sneaking into the yard behind my back,' Janus said.

'No,' Pier said, stepping back a little, 'so I could quickly stuff them full of cherries.'

Amazingly, Janus threw his head back and roared with laughter. 'That's it,' he said at last. 'Now that's more like it. I was wondering what had happened to you kids this spring—not a kid after my cherries, just those miserable starlings and all those other sneaky birds. Now and then a magpie. There's an honest bird for you; he's willing to risk his neck for a cherry or two. But not a kid! You're the first two. But I see now. You had wagon wheels on the brain.'

'Well,' Pier said, 'we almost made it.'

Dirk gave Pier a hard warning nudge.

'Yep,' Janus said mildly enough, 'I've got to admit it. You'd have made it if you hadn't yelled out to save your brother.'

'I had to,' Pier said. 'I couldn't let you smash his hand.'

'Did you think I would?' Janus said, startled. 'No, kid. I'm afraid I think too much of hands and legs to want to smash anybody's. Is that what you kids tell each other about me?'

Pier was embarrassed. He looked down and stared hard at the wheel of Janus's chair.

'Storks, huh?' Janus abruptly changed the subject. 'Now there's an honest bird for you, too, and no mean cherry robber. I would like to see storks sailing over the roofs of Shora again, but not a wagon wheel anywhere, you say? Well, I haven't got one for you either. All the wheels I've got are on this chair. Hey!' he suddenly yelled at Pier, 'don't look at that wheel so hard. You weren't thinking of robbing a poor legless man of a wheel off his wheel chair, were you?'

'They're too small,' Pier said promptly.

Janus laughed. 'So you were thinking about it?'

Pier came a little closer. 'Janus,' he asked earnestly. 'Were both your legs bitten off by a shark in one bite?'

Janus looked startled. 'Is that what you kids tell each other about me?' he demanded.

Pier flushed. Dirk nudged him warningly from behind. But Pier could only plunge on now. 'Yes,' he said, 'and they say that's what makes you so fierce.' Suddenly he realized what he had said. 'Not that I . . . Well, I know I'd be fierce, too, without any legs,' he said, red to the roots of his red hair. 'I thought about it, and I sort of think I know just how it feels, and . . .' His voice faded away; he had no words for it. It would be silly to explain to Janus the make-believe, scary things he had imagined at the side of the road.

'Oh, you do,' Janus said. He looked strangely at Pier. 'You're an odd one. So you'd be fierce, too? Well, maybe I wouldn't feel so fierce if they had been bitten off by a shark. That would be something to think back on and sort of boast about. But it wasn't a shark. My legs were bitten off by a mosquito.'

Dirk laughed an unbelieving little laugh. Pier goggled at the man.

'Honest,' Janus said simply. 'One little miserable mosquito bit me one night, both legs, while I was sleeping. I must have scratched the bites and got blood poisoning. And I didn't go to a doctor. Sort of scared of doctors, I was. And then they had to cut them off.'

'Oh, golly, Janus,' Dirk said.

But Pier suddenly turned and hurried to the cherry tree. When he gave the rope a sudden yank, the whole tree flashed and clanked and jangled. 'I always wanted to do that,' Pier said in an odd, strangled little voice. Then he came back to Janus's chair. 'You really wouldn't have smashed Dirk's hand with that stone, would you?' he demanded.

The man glared at him. 'You kids tell each other *that*! No, I wouldn't. All I wanted was to see his face

55

coming over the wall with me sitting there ready with a stone. No, I think too much of hands and arms and legs. It's just some little queer fun I have—scaring birds and making kids' livers turn over. It's a little something.'

Then Pier stepped solemnly before him and said, 'I don't like your story about the mosquito, and it doesn't sound true like the shark. Didn't he say, Dirk, that if a shark had bitten off his legs he wouldn't be fierce? Janus isn't fierce.'

'Oh, golly, no,' Dirk said fervently. 'Jella must have made up a lot of it,' he told Pier, 'just to show us how brave he was.'

But the man was looking oddly at Pier. 'So you want it to be a shark? I'd have a right to be fierce if it had been a miserable little mosquito, but since it was a man-sized shark, I've no call to be fierce. Is that it?'

Pier looked right at Janus and nodded and nodded. 'I think so. I think that's the way it must be, because you aren't fierce at all. Don't you think so, Dirk?'

'Oh, golly, yes,' Dirk said.

They stood there a little awkwardly, not knowing what more to say. They turned toward the gate. A little red-faced and uneasy they started to move off. 'We've got to hurry and look some more for a wheel,' Pier explained.

Then he and Dirk turned back to the gate. The gate had opened wide before them! Janus laughed. 'Rigged that up with ropes, too,' he said proudly.

The boys stood there, wanting to tell Janus things but finding no words to express the amazing surprise inside of them. Janus had become real; he had become a part of their village. He wasn't a fearsome ogre to be hated and outwitted. Even the yard with its forbidding high fence somehow looked different now. Lina could have told Pier and Dirk what it was. Lina would have said that it was just that Janus had become important, in the same way that old Grandmother Sibble III had become real and important. He had become a friend!

But Pier and Dirk had no words for it. They still dawdled at the gate. Pier, no doubt, would have come up with something, but just then there was a yell from the street. There stood Eelka and a soaked, dripping Jella with their arms full of spokes and rim sections.

'Eelka and Jella've got a wheel!' Pier yelled at Janus.

CHAPTER VI

Eelka and
the Ancient Wheel

EELKA had been given the canal road to search. It was an important road that followed the canal all the way to the village of Hantum. Eelka did not expect to get to Hantum; the canal road had far too many farms. He searched each farm in his own slow, thorough way. Bit by bit he worked himself far out of Shora. In his own way, Eelka hurried.

At the end of a bush-lined lane that led to a huge ancient farmhouse, a young farmer suddenly stepped from behind the bushes and barred Eelka's way. 'And just what are you snooping around for? Saw you at the next farm, too. Just what business did you have nosing around that farm with nobody at home?'

'Oh,' Eelka said, startled. He eyed the tall farmer, wondering if it would be wise to take to his heels, but quickly decided there wouldn't be much use in *his* running away. He tried a slow, sure smile instead. 'Oh, I wasn't exactly snooping,' he told the farmer as calmly as he could. 'I was looking for a wagon wheel. Have you got a spare wagon wheel?'

'Huh?' the farmer said. It was his turn to be startled.

'You see,' Eelka explained, 'our school needs a wagon wheel, because we're trying to make the storks come back to Shora. The whole school's doing it . . .' Eelka explained the big plans and the project.

His calm, slow, thorough explanation seemed to satisfy the farmer. 'Well, now,' he said, 'it must be Providence or something. To keep an eye on you on that next farm, I climbed into the hayloft of our old second barn. We haven't used that hayloft since my great-grandfather's days, but what do you think? There's an old wagon wheel there! If it's a year old, it's a hundred. I didn't know it was there. I wouldn't have found it now, but running to the little window to keep an eye on you, I tripped over the thing. It was buried under old hay. Skinned my ankles, too! I can tell you I didn't feel too good about your making me go on my face into that dust and dead hay.'

'Golly, no,' Eelka said. He eyed the tall farmer warily. Three long strides and the farmer would have him if he ran. 'Well, I can't say I'm glad that happened, but I *am* glad you found the wheel if I can have it.'

The farmer grinned. 'That's certainly putting it the straightforward way! I suppose you can have it—no reason why not. It's so old and big and clumsy it wouldn't fit any of our wagons today.'

'You mean I can have it just like that?' Eelka had to ask again. It was too simple and too easy after his long hard search.

'If you can get it down, you can have it. It's no good to anybody here.'

Eelka eyed the high barn. He pointed to two double

doors high in the front gable of the barn, directly under the peak of the roof. 'Is that where it is? Way up there? Could I get it through the hay doors and let it down with a rope?'

The farmer studied the barn. 'Yes, if you open both doors. That's the way it must have got in, because the trap door inside the loft is far too small. You'd have to get help, though. You can see I'm all dressed up. I was ready to set out for Hantum when I first saw you down the road, and I'm very late now from hanging around to keep an eye on you. I wouldn't try it alone. That wheel's heavy, and if you try letting it down with a rope, it's liable to take you down with it. You can see it's pretty high.'

'Could I go up just to look at it?'

'Well,' the farmer hesitated. 'The men are all out on the farm—nobody around . . . Well, go ahead, but didn't you say the whole school was at it? Better get the whole school to help you. I wouldn't try it alone. But I've got to get to Hantum!' Abruptly the farmer set off down the lane.

Halfway down the lane, the farmer turned. 'I'll take a chance on you. Fat, slow kids are usually pretty honest. They have to be; they can't run away. So I expect you to leave things alone in that barn. But the wheel is yours. Go right ahead.' He was off again.

Eelka stood staring up at the barn, wondering whether to get the others to help or to try it all alone. Imagine his coming rolling a big wheel to the school all alone! They'd never thought he could do much of anything, because he was so fat and slow and clumsy. Wouldn't their eyes pop! Eelka's own eyes popped as he imagined the picture. He hurried into the barn. Imagine it, if he could be the one to bring the wheel to school!

Eelka climbed heavily up the long, rickety, dried-out ladder that led to the high hayloft. The ladder

60

groaned and squeaked under him. Eelka was puffing when he pushed his head through the little trap door opening. There it was. There lay the wheel! It lay deep and heavy and ponderous among the age-old hay settlings on the floor of the hayloft. It was exposed. The scrambled markings in the hay-dust settlings where the farmer had sprawled full-length were all around it. Panting as much from excitement as from the hard climb, Eelka stood over it. He had a wheel! It was his! His for the lowering, his for the rolling it back to school. Maybe they'd all be standing empty-handed in the playground when he came rolling up with the wheel!

But this was no time to dream about it and make great proud pictures in his head. Eelka hurried to the double doors, unhooked them, and fiercely pushed them open. They slammed against the outside wall. Now there was light. He hurried back to the wheel to examine it by the new light. He felt solemn, looking down at a century-old wheel—the farmer had said it was a hundred, if it was a year. He prodded it with his toe. He felt solemn and excited all at the same time, here in the deep silence of the ancient barn.

From a crossbeam above him dangled the end of a heavy rope. That must be the hay rope they had used to pull the hay into this loft. Maybe it was a hundred years old, too. It was Providence, just as the farmer had said. Not only did he have a wheel but there was the rope to lower it down to the ground. Eelka hitched himself up the smooth upright beam to get to the rope on the crossbeam. The farmer hadn't said anything about using the rope, but he would know a rope was needed to lower the wheel to the ground.

Eelka dragged himself cautiously along the cross-beam around which the old rope had been coiled. From his high perch he saw the wheel directly below him. His wheel! He hesitated no longer, uncoiled the

61

rope, loosened the knot, and let it drop down on the wheel. He slid down the upright beam and hastily tied one end of the rope around the rim of the wheel. He dragged the wheel flat on its hub across the gritty floor to the hay door opening.

On hands and knees Eelka leaned out of the high barn. He gasped a little. It looked twice as high from the open doorway as it had from the ground below. Eelka eyed the long rope on the hayloft floor. He decided it must be plenty long enough to let the wheel down to the ground—far as it seemed. But could he do it? Could he hold it when all its heavy weight hung outside the barn, dangling from the end of a rope? From his high post in the hay door opening, Eelka stared over the flat countryside, hoping, wishing there was somebody to help him. Far away across the level fields he could just see the sharp roof of Shora's little school. Maybe it would be better to get the others. Suddenly a commotion on a distant road caught Eelka's eye. Wasn't that Jella? It was! Jella had a wheel! He was rolling a wheel toward the school. Jella had beaten him as always. In utter disappointment Eelka stared at the rolling wheel on the distant road.

Then from his height Eelka saw the farmer, saw him sneaking along the bank of a ditch that ran beside the road down which Jella was rolling the wheel. Eelka yelled, yelled with all his might to warn Jella. Jella didn't hear him; the distance was too great. The farmer grabbed Jella. Jella's wheel went wobbling off the side of the road and down into the ditch. Now the farmer led Jella away down the road toward the school. 'Oh, oh,' Eelka said softly, 'Jella stole that wheel!'

He stared after Jella and the farmer. He shook his head, but somehow deep inside him he felt a certain satisfaction. Jella was always the leader and was always scolding him for being slow and clumsy and coming in behind. Jella didn't even want him in his games most of the time. But now if he could get this big wheel down, he'd be the leader! For once he'd be the leader. All Eelka's misgivings flitted away before his new determination for once to outdo Jella.

Eelka did not look back at Jella again. He was determined. He pushed the wheel out of the open doorway as far as he dared but not so far that it would overbalance and shoot down to the ground. Now the wheel lay ready to be lowered. Eelka studied the situation. Maybe it would be best to tie the other end of the rope around his chest. That would leave his hands free, in case he had to grab and hang on to something to keep the wheel from pulling him out of the high hayloft.

With the rope knotted around his chest, Eelka took the precaution of walking around the same upright beam he had climbed to get the rope. With the rope going around the beam, the big wheel would not have a direct pull. If the wheel should drag him, it would first have to pull him across the floor away from the doorway and clear around the upright beam. The rope proved to be long enough so that Eelka could walk around the beam with it and still get back to the open doorway where the wheel lay.

Eelka did not hesitate now. With his foot he gave the wheel a hard shove. The big wheel teetered for a moment, tipped down, and shot out of the high doorway.

Behind Eelka the slack rope snaked and became taut. With a terrific yank Eelka was jerked off his feet. He fell backward, flat on his back. The flying rope dragged him through dust and stalks toward the upright beam. Eelka had sense enough to put out his hands to keep from crashing headfirst into the beam. For a moment he clung to the smooth beam, but the speed of the falling wheel outside the barn jerked him around the beam, twisted him so that now he was flat on his face, and tore his hands free before he could get a secure hold. Eelka shot across the hayloft floor toward the wide-open doorway. There was nothing to grab. He clutched wildly at the hay stalks. There was nothing to slow him. Eelka sprawled his legs wide in a desperate effort to slow himself. His hands clawed at the rope around his chest. He frantically tried to undo the knot. There was no time. There was the open doorway. Eelka grabbed blindly and dug nails and fingers into the old dead wood of the door jamb. Somehow he held. The weight of the wheel spun him around. As he clung with his hands, his feet went out of the doorway.

For an unbelievable and horrible moment Eelka hung. His shoes flew off his feet, and because the moment seemed so long, it seemed to take time before he heard his shoes hit the hard-packed ground below. He scrabbled for a stronger, surer hold on the worn door jamb. Then a horrible yank shook through his whole body. The rope wasn't long enough. The wheel was hanging above the ground, hanging from him like an awful pendulum. The rope around his chest slipped down. There was a brief, blind moment of hope that it would slip right down his dangling legs and off him. But the rope caught around Eelka's thick waist.

Eelka hung by his fingers. Far below him, suspended from him by the thick old rope, the wheel dangled against the wall of the barn.

These were blinding short moments; there could not be many more moments. He could never hold the wheel, hanging as he was by his hands. Eelka closed his eyes. His breath retched out of him. All he could do was cling another moment of eternity and, if possible, yet another.

At that point the rope broke. The wheel crashed below. The strain was gone, the strain on his waist and clutching fingers. Suddenly there was breath again and a feeling of heavenly lightness, as if he were flying, as if he could fly. And with new strength Eelka tugged himself up and dragged himself up through the doorway. When his legs were safely in the loft, he stretched full-length in the dust and stalks and sobbed. He lay flat, his breath rattling out of him. It was good to lie and sob, never to have to stir again.

Then Eelka remembered the crashing sound the wheel had made. Slowly, timidly, flat on the floor, he put his head out of the doorway. He just lay and stared. There was the wheel, smashed into a hundred pieces. Only the iron rim with its inside wooden rim had stayed together. The big hub had rolled away; the spokes lay scattered in every direction.

Eelka groaned. His narrow escape was forgotten in his utter disappointment. The wheel was all in pieces. Gone was the proud vision of rolling the wheel to school. Eelka slowly got up. He pulled the two hay doors shut and remembered to latch them. Without bothering to undo the piece of broken rope, still knotted around his waist, he went down the long ladder, staring blank-faced at nothing.

The wreckage was complete. Eelka looked gloomily at the shattered wheel before him. He picked up his wooden shoes, examined them to see if they had split, then slid them on his feet. He turned to go but looked back. Could the wheel be put together again? He still had all the parts!

He started gathering up the scattered spokes. They made a staggering armful. There was still the hub, and if he was to roll the rim away, he would need both his hands. Eelka pondered. The rope still knotted around his waist provided a solution. One by one he shoved the spokes under the tight rope around his waist until he was ringed by spokes. He had to walk very straight. He could hardly stoop to pick up the heavy hub. But what to do with the hub? He couldn't carry it in his hands, because his hands had to be kept free to roll the rim to Shora. Walking stiffly in his clumsy corset of wheel spokes, Eelka went to the rope that lay over the rim. By jerking and snapping the old rope he broke it. It unravelled and parted strand by strand. Now he had a short length of rope. He tied it around the hub, lowered the hub carefully over his shoulder, and tied the other end to the rope still knotted around his waist. There, that solved the problem of the hub! Now the rim—— He could hardly reach down to it, encased as he was in wheel spokes. At last he got it off the ground and standing upright.

Harnessed in spokes, the heavy hub unwieldy on his back, Eelka got the rim rolling. He trotted stiffly beside it. Down the farm lane the wheel rim rolled very nicely, but on the rutted canal road it developed a mean tendency to bump down into one of the two

wagon ruts or to hit pebbles and suddenly veer toward the deep canal. Eelka couldn't move quickly. He could do only one thing. Whenever the rim veered toward the canal, he knocked it flat before it could plunge into the water. The straining, struggling Eelka was soon drenched with sweat. He grunted and panted. But always he picked the rim up again and rolled it on, determined somehow to get it to the school.

He got better at managing the jumpy rim. He found that by keeping it in one of the deep wagon ruts of the canal road, the rut made a sort of track for the rim. Now he was beginning to make progress. The rim rolled down the rut; the loaded Eelka trotted beside. At this pace they'd soon be in Shora.

The iron rim rolling beside Eelka suddenly hit a big pebble in the rut and bounced up. To Eelka's relief it bounced right back down into the rut. Then all in one moment the whole rim came apart! The inner wooden rim had come loose from the outer iron rim. The wooden rim had been made out of short fitted sections, and now that one of the sections had let go, the whole rim fell to pieces. The sections clattered down and lay scattered along the road. Eelka stopped. He stood and stared in dismay at the trail of wooden rim sections. The iron outer rim rolled on by itself.

There was a loud shout across a field. 'Watch it. Watch that rim!' Eelka threw a startled glance at the field. It was Jella, running toward him and shouting. Eelka whirled toward the iron rim. It was too late to do anything. The rim had jumped up out of the rut and had rolled across the road. There was a splash as the rim disappeared in the canal.

Eelka's heart sank, but he ran to the canal. A stiff anger rose in him—if Jella hadn't shouted! He angrily undid the rope that held the heavy hub over his shoulder and let it drop. He looked at it as if he had a mind to kick it in the canal. Down the steep bank in the canal, the bottom mud came wheeling up where the iron rim had sunk. A few dirty bubbles came to the surface and broke.

'Keep your eye on the spot and don't move!' Jella came yelling across the road. 'What'd you let it go in the canal for?'

Eelka stared bitterly at the water. 'It came apart,' he managed to say. 'It fell into pieces.' He pointed to the trail of wooden rim sections on the road.

Jella looked at the clouded water. 'Is that where it went in?'

Eelka nodded. All of a sudden he was too close to tears to trust his voice. He'd worked so hard, and now . . . Suddenly he was angry again. He hadn't noticed until now, but Jella had his bow with him; he even had arrows for it. Jella had been fooling around with a bow and arrows. But Eelka said nothing.

Jella carefully laid his arrows down. Now he stretched flat on the bank and poked with his bow down into the murky water. He got up on hands and knees. 'I can't reach it with my bow.' He looked up at Eelka. 'Can you swim?'

'No, can you?'

'No, but I was thinking.' Jella looked at Eelka encased in his wheel spokes, then at the hub lying on the canal bank. 'Hey! You could let me down by the rope on that hub.'

For answer Eelka picked up the rope and yanked at one of the end strands. The strand ravelled apart and broke in his fingers. 'Golly, no,' Jella said. 'I'd be for the fishes.'

'We've got to get help,' Eelka said.

'Yes, but then we'd maybe lose the spot where the rim went down. Hey, I know!' Jella exclaimed. 'Look, we'll use those spokes you've got around you. We'll drive them in the canal bank like stakes, like a sort of a ladder going down to the water. Then I can let myself down into the water by hanging from the bottom stake. I can feel with my toes for the rim. Look, we'll use that hub as a sort of sledge hammer to drive the stakes in.'

'That iron rim 's awfully heavy,' Eelka said doubtfully. 'You couldn't pull it up with your toes.'

But Jella was so absorbed in his plan, he paid no attention. He untied the rope from the hub and drove the first spoke down into the perpendicular bank of the canal. A foot or so lower he drove a second one. 'Hand me another,' he panted. He drove the third spoke into the bank, then he couldn't reach any lower. 'Your turn,' Jella said. 'Look, I'll hold you by your ankles, and you can hang down the bank and drive in the lower spokes.'

It was almost impossible to drive stakes into the bank while hanging upside down. The blood rushed to Eelka's head. The hub was almost too heavy to hold with one hand until he had the stake started so he could hammer at the stake with both hands. Eelka managed to drive in a spoke. It scared him horribly when Jella let go one leg and picked up a spoke to hand down to him. As Jella stooped with the spoke, Eelka slid a little farther down the bank, a little closer to the water. It unnerved him. He managed to tap the spoke into the bank with the hub, but everything swam before his eyes. 'I can't any more upside down,' he said. The awkward hub slid from his nerveless hand, plunged in the canal, and disappeared.

'Aw, you clumsy fathead!' Jella angrily said as he dragged Eelka up the bank. 'Now the hub 's gone too. Can't you ever do anything right?'

On hands and knees Eelka painfully crawled away from the canal's edge and sat down in the grass. Everything spun; everything was cloudy before his eyes. He sat dazed. He hardly knew or cared that a cloudy, dim Jella had suddenly vanished from the canal bank.

69

There wasn't a sound. Suddenly it scared Eelka. He crawled back to the canal's edge and peered down. He shook his head, shook it again to clear his vision. There hung Jella by one of the spokes driven into the bank. He was down in the water, feeling with his toes for the rim. The clouds of mud he was stirring up were welling and circling around him.

Jella saw him. 'Don't feel a thing,' he said. 'But I can go deeper.' He eyed the bottom spoke. 'If I hang from that last spoke, I can go away under and feel for the rim.'

'I don't know,' Eelka said. 'I wouldn't, Jella. I don't think I hit it very hard before I dropped the hub.'

But Jella was already gone, all of him, except the hand that clutched the bottom spoke. Eelka stared into the rising mud clouds. Filthy black bubbles broke with a little sound. It made Eelka panicky. He looked at the stake the hand was clutching.

Then to Eelka's utter relief Jella rose and dragged himself up by the stake, blowing and snorting and spitting. 'Didn't feel a thing,' he said. 'Got to go still deeper.' And down he started again!

'No, Jella, no!' Eelka yelled.

But Jella started to sink away just the same.

'Jella, don't!'

'I'm not,' Jella said queerly. 'I don't want to . . .' He gulped, struggled up wildly for a moment, and got his mouth above water. 'Eelka, I'm going!'

Eelka's horrified eyes flew from Jella to the spoke in the bank. The spoke wasn't in the bank! It was in Jella's hand! In a moment the stake in Jella's sinking hand would be gone, too, under the muddy water. Jella was going down with the loose stake! Eelka threw himself down the bank, down the little ladder of spokes. He clung to what was now the last spoke. He let himself drop into the water. Clinging fiercely to the stake, he kicked out at what he could still see of the spoke in Jella's hand. Jella felt the kick, and his hand clutched, grabbed, clung. With Jella dragging behind through the water, Eelka pulled himself up the spoke ladder, up by his hands for Jella had a drowning hold on both his legs now. Eelka couldn't use his feet. Hand over hand up the ladder of spokes, Eelka dragged Jella up after him out of the water. His desperate strength seemed endless; it was enough for anything. Below him Jella suddenly cried, 'Eelka, get off, get off. They're all going!'

Eelka threw a scared glance down. Then Jella let go. Eelka threw himself up the bank. He grabbed the first thing that came to his hand—Jella's bow lying there. He poked the bow down to the wild-eyed Jella. Jella grabbed it. Eelka pulled Jella against the bank and held him there.

'Can you pull me up with the bow?' Jella gasped.

Eelka shook his head. Suddenly his fierce strength was all gone, and he was scared. There hung Jella in the water. There hung the spokes, all but the top one loose, almost dangling in the bank. He'd come up by those with Jella hanging on to him as a dead weight. The only spoke still straight and firm was the first one Jella had pounded into the top of the dry bank. Suddenly Eelka took his end of the bow and hung it around the stake. He jumped to his feet.

'Jella,' he said desperately. 'I've got to get help. I don't dare try to pull you up by that bow. What if it would break?' He looked all around but there was no one near. No one. Nothing moved. 'Jella,' he said, 'will you hang there very still? Don't put any strain on the bow; don't stir. Will you, Jella? Then I'll run to Shora and get help.'

'Well, run then,' Jella said desperately. 'Don't stand there talking about it. Run.' His big scared eyes stared up at Eelka.

'I will, I will, Jella,' Eelka cried. But it seemed

71

almost impossible to get started. It was an awful feeling to run away, leaving Jella behind in the still canal. 'I'm going,' Eelka said. He turned and ran.

He ran hard. He had to run hard to run away from Jella. Now Jella was back there alone in the quiet canal. Jella was back there and scared.

Eelka glanced about him, but there was no help anywhere. Nothing moved. The road lay empty. The canal lay silent and empty. And Jella was in the canal.

Suddenly Eelka wasn't running any more. He stood dead still in the empty silence. He couldn't run away from Jella—Jella was scared. Jella, who wasn't supposed to be scared of anything, was horribly scared.

Suddenly it struck Eelka. He could pull Jella up out of the canal! The rope would hold Jella! The rope had to hold. It had held the wheel for a long time, and the wheel must have been ten times heavier than Jella. He could pull Jella out, because not only had the rope held the wheel, he had held up the enormous wheel while hanging by almost nothing but his finger tips.

It startled Eelka. He was running back, and he was startled—because he knew he was strong. He might be slow and fat, but he was strong. Much stronger than anybody knew, much stronger than he himself had ever suspected. Hadn't he held the wheel? Hadn't he dragged Jella up until the spokes in the bank gave way? He must be ten times stronger than he'd ever known!

He was back at the spot on the canal and was peering over the edge down at Jella.

'Oh, you're back quick,' Jella said gratefully.

'I didn't go,' Eelka said. 'I came back. I'm going to pull you out now.'

'How?' Jella asked anxiously.

But Eelka had no time for talk. He knotted the two pieces of rope together, the one from his waist and the one from the hub. He tested his knot. Then he tied a slipknot in the end, made a big loop, and dropped it over Jella's head. Now he tested the lone spoke in the top of the bank. He braced one foot against it after kicking off his wooden shoe to get a secure hold against the stake.

'Now,' he ordered Jella, 'let the rope slide down over one arm, then hang on to the bow with the other hand, and let it slide over the other arm. Easy,' he warned. 'Do it slowly. Don't jerk around and get panicky.'

Jella obeyed. He moved cautiously, not putting any unnecessary strain on the bow as he changed positions. The moment the rope loop dropped over Jella's chest, Eelka drew it tight. 'Now,' he said, 'I'm starting to pull you up. Don't struggle; hang like a sack.'

'But the rope 's no good. That strand just came apart like a hair a while ago.' Jella was scared.

'The *whole* rope will hold you. It held the wheel when I let it down out of a high barn, and that wheel is ten times heavier than you. And I can do it. If I could let down that wheel, I can pull you up.'

He made himself sound much surer than he felt for Jella's sake, because Jella was scared.

'But, Eelka——'

'Don't talk,' Eelka said shortly. 'Up you come now.' He planted his foot against the spoke. Hand over hand he began tugging the rope up. Hand over hand, all his weight against the stake, not dragging and grinding the poor weak rope against the bank's edge. Eelka set his teeth. While Jella had been in the water, it had gone easy, but now all of Jella's weight hung from his arms. But keep the rope clear of the bank; don't let it grind. Hand over hand, just pull, pull, pull.

Suddenly there was no weight. For an awful moment Eelka expected to hear the sound of a splash again—the rope must have broken. But there was no splash. Jella had grabbed the spoke in the top of the bank,

and now he flung himself up. He threw his legs up and around and rolled over and over away from the canal.

Eelka suddenly lay down. It felt wonderful to lie there, knowing he had done it—done what he had intended to do and done it just as he had planned. He had been strong; the rope hadn't broken. It was a wonderful proud feeling.

Jella had got up and now he leaned over Eelka. 'Golly, Eelka, I never knew you were so strong.'

'I didn't, either,' Eelka said, looking up at Jella. 'I was just thinking about it. I suppose that's what comes of being the baby of the family. They think you stay

74

little. I must just have believed them. My dad and big brothers, they always did things before I could, because I was little. I was the baby.'

'Some baby,' Jella said gratefully.

Suddenly they grinned at each other. But it was awkward. Jella didn't know how to say how grateful he was. Eelka could almost see him poking around in his mind for the words. They grinned at each other again.

'Golly, Eelka, you may be slow, but I never knew you were that strong! You can be in our games all right—that strong . . .'

Eelka knew it was Jella's way of thanking him. He jumped up. 'You know I was thinking—— We'd better grab up all the spokes and rim sections and take them to school and tell teacher. We'll leave that one spoke in the bank for a marker, so we'll know the place. Then maybe with a long rake we can drag for the rim and pull out the hub, too.'

Jella obediently went to the road to gather up the scattered rim sections. Eelka piled the thick spokes on one arm. Together they went down the road to Shora, dripping water wtih every step. Every now and then big Jella looked at short, fat Eelka trudging sturdily along beside him. He shook his head as if he still could not quite believe it.

'Some baby!' he suddenly said out loud. And Eelka grinned.

CHAPTER VII

Auka and
the Tin Man

AUKA had been given the dike road to search. The dike road led to the village of Nes. With Lina on top of the dike and Auka on the road below, it was pleasant going for a while. They shouted back and forth to each other. From the dike Lina was supposed to spy out the little side roads and lanes that led to the back farms lying off the main roads.

'I'm going all the way to Nes,' Auka shouted up at her. 'Maybe even all through Nes.'

'Wish I could go with you,' Lina called back enviously.

'Why?'

'Oh, those back farms sometimes have great big watchdogs. And I'm scared of dogs.'

'They won't hurt you,' Auka assured her. 'Just look them straight in the eye and keep walking right up to them.'

'Which eye?' Lina asked from the top of the dike. She giggled nervously.

'You want me to take the side roads and you take my road to Nes?' Auka offered.

'No-oo, I think not,' Lina called back doubtfully. 'There are more houses on your road, and the more houses the more dogs. At least from the dike I can spy out if there's a dog in the yard and if he's alone or if there are people around. I'll just go singing all the way down those lanes so the dogs can hear me coming.'

'You mean you don't want to take them by surprise and maybe scare them half to death?' Auka teased.

Lina made a face at him.

On the road below the dike Auka reached the first farmhouse. The house stood at a curve in the dike road. From there the road turned away from the sea and the dike to the inland village of Nes. Nes had trees and Nes had storks. Auka was anxious to get there.

When Auka reappeared from his search of the yard and the barns, Lina was nowhere in sight. Later when Auka passed a narrow lane he heard faint singing around a curve. It must be Lina. Auka barked hoarsely.

Lina heard him through her singing. He could hear her laugh nervously.

'Hope you find a dozen wheels and no dogs,' Auka shouted to the unseen Lina. Then he hurried on.

Auka was nearing Nes at last. His trip so far had been fruitless. Not a farm had a wheel to spare. Across a flat field the roofs of Nes among green trees blinked warm and red in the sun. Auka rested awhile on the side of the road near a narrow dirt lane, hoping that Lina might be down that lane. He listened in the country quiet for any sound of singing. A thin, rattling jangling sound came to his ears from the depths of the bush-lined lane. Auka listened and grinned. It must be Lina.

She must have grown tired of singing and must

be rattling something now to warn the dogs of her approach.

The faint jangling noise seemed to be drawing closer. It was hard to tell. It kept stopping and then starting up again. Now it had stopped. After a long silence, the jangling began again and drew steadily closer. At last Auka thought he knew what it was. It must be the tinware peddler with shiny, tinny pots and pans and kettles hanging from hooks and wires all over his wagon. It *was* the tin man. Down the narrow lane a skinny old horse came slowly into sight and behind him was the jangling wagon. But there was no one on the seat! One side of the wagon was completely off the road, running in the roadside grass. It must be that the old horse had decided to go home and had left the tin man behind at some farm.

The wagon stopped, and Auka saw the tin man come around the back of the wagon. He fussed with the back wheel that had been running in the grass. Auka waited. At last the tin man mounted the high seat, and the wagon came on again.

The old wagon came grinding and rattling out of the lane. It made a wide, careful turn into the road where Auka was standing. The hub of the wheel almost grazed Auka, but still the tin man had not noticed him. The man sat twisted in the seat, his eyes fixed on the back wheel of the wagon.

Auka looked at the wheel. 'Hey, your rim is coming off!'

The tin man started, saw Auka, and hastily stopped his horse.

'Your wheel—it's coming apart,' Auka yelled at him again.

'Yes, I know. I know,' the man said morosely, 'I've been holding the rim in place with wires all the way from Shora, but the wires wear through so soon. Then I have to twist new ones around the rim again to hold

it on the wheel.' He climbed down wearily, hunted a wire out of the back of his wagon, and wrapped it around the rim. There were wires twisted around the whole rim every few inches.

'Why don't you give me the wheel?' Auka suddenly said. 'It's no good.'

'That's a funny thing to say,' the tin man said reprovingly. 'Give it to you? And what am I supposed to do then? Ride home on the axle?'

Auka realized he had been abrupt in blurting out his odd demand. He hastily explained to the tin man the stork plans the school had for Shora and the need for a wheel.

'Well, there's no doubt that's all it's good for— storks,' the tin man said. 'But I'm going to need it until I get another wheel. As soon as I get to Nes, I'm just going to have to get another one, that's sure.'

'Oh, then may I go with you?' Auka asked eagerly.

'I'm going to Nes, too. Then when you get the new wheel and if I could have the old one . . . It would be fine for storks,' he explained earnestly. 'It doesn't have to roll for storks, and storks wouldn't mind a few wires. So long as they don't catch their toes in them.'

'Not so fast, not so fast,' the tin man said. 'I need a new wheel, I've got to get a new wheel, but how I'm going to get one is something else again. It's been a sorry week. All I did was patch a few pots and pans on my route. Hardly a soul bought anything new. In that whole dump of Shora, only that legless fellow bought some scrap pieces of tin. Said he wanted to hang them in a tree. But that's all I sold in Shora.'

'Oh, that was Janus,' Auka said. 'They're to scare the birds out of his cherry tree.' His eyes brightened. 'Hey, that must mean the cherries are going to start to turn red!'

The tin man didn't listen but clucked the old horse ahead a few steps. He carefully studied the turning wheel. Even the spaced wires weren't keeping the outer metal rim in place on the wooden rim of the wheel. In a few turnings of the wheel, the wires stretched and allowed the outer rim to run almost halfway off the wheel. When the wheel turned, the iron rim sort of wobbled beside the wooden rim that it was supposed to cover. The man surveyed the gravel road. 'You can see the roofs of Nes,' he said hopelessly, 'but on that gravel I'll be winding wire so much, it'll be dark before I get there.'

'If I got on the back of the wagon and the moment I saw a wire giving out I quickly twisted on another wire,' Auka suggested, 'then you wouldn't have to stop and get down all the time.'

'Well,' the man said, 'that's an idea. That way we might both get to Nes. But remember, I can't promise you that wheel.' He handed Auka a handful of short

80

pieces of wire and helped boost him into the high wagon.

Tinware was hanging everywhere. Auka had to push pots and pans and kettles aside like a curtain before he could put his head out to watch the wagon wheel.

'Just shout "whoa" whenever you see a wire going,' the tin man instructed as he climbed back to his seat.

'Will your horse hear me when everything's rattling and banging?' Auka asked doubtfully.

'Him? He could hear "whoa" ten feet under water. But "gee-up", that he doesn't understand very well. Gee-up!' he told the horse.

'If you do get a new wheel, may I have the old one?' Auka hastily bargained before the wagon could get into motion when the rattling of the tin would drown him out.

'We'll have to see if my wife has a little money left from last week. I sure didn't earn enough this week to buy as much as a spoke. Gee-up!' he told the horse again.

'But what'll you do if your wife hasn't?' Auka asked. 'It's sure you can't go out with this wheel next week.'

'Oh, I'll just throw it in the canal over Sunday to soak and swell. Then it's good for a couple of days, and if we get some rain, that helps, too. But this whole week was dry as cork. Gee-up!' the tin man patiently repeated. 'But I'm afraid it's gone too far this time. I'm afraid even soaking won't help it.' He spread his hands wide. 'But what can you do without money? Gee-up, I said!'

The old horse seemed to sense that the conversation had definitely ended. He unwillingly got into bony, clumsy motion. The wagon creaked ahead. The tin began to jiggle and rattle and jangle.

Nes wasn't far, but even in that short distance Auka

became very handy at wrapping wires around the old, tired, warped wheel. He soon got so he could almost tell when a worn wire was going to snap. The old horse moved so slowly Auka could give the wire a single wrap around the rim, wait for it to come back up again, and then twist it tightly into place. He seldom had to shout 'whoa', but when he did, the old horse—in spite of all the jangling of the tin—stopped before the word was out of Auka's mouth. He almost seemed to know when Auka was starting to think 'whoa'.

On the sharp gravel road, wires gave way right and left. Auka was busy as a bee, and it was rather fun to see if he could get a wire around the rim without having to stop the old horse. Besides, there was the hope this might get him a wagon wheel for the roof of the school. You could never tell. It seemed more hopeful than going around to the farms. Not a farmer seemed to have a wheel that wasn't on a wagon.

At last they rode down the cobbled street of Nes. Auka took time from his busy wire twisting to look up at a huge white stork rising from the roof of a house. It flapped away as a second stork came winging back to the nest on the roof. The storks were already building nests in Nes! Auka had to tear his eyes away from the storks; even in that brief time five wires had broken loose from the rim. Auka had to shout to the horse. He replaced three of the wires, then he noticed that he had no more. The last wire had been used on the wheel.

'No more wires,' he told the tin man. 'Finished.'

'So am I,' the tin man said. 'I gave you all the wires I had in the wagon, but it just has to hold to the end of this street. That's where I live.'

The wires didn't last. One after the other they wore away on the cobblestones. Now not a single wire was left. The iron rim threatened to come right off.

'How far yet?' Auka asked.

The tin man stopped and looked at the wheel. Silently he handed Auka a hammer he used in his trade. 'Would you walk beside the wagon and just pound the rim back whenever it starts to roll off? I'll try to pick out the smoothest places in the street.'

Auka jumped down and took the hammer. He pounded the rim back on the wheel. 'Go ahead now,' he said. The wagon rolled ahead. The slow wheel, with Auka stalking beside it, hobbled over the cobblestones. Auka watched it like a hawk, and whenever the iron rim threatened to leave the wheel, he slapped it back with the hammer. To the tinny rattle of the pots and pans as the wagon bounced along the street were now added the hard sounds of Auka's constant hammering. It was a miserable din. Children along the street started to follow the wagon.

The wagon stopped before a little house. They had arrived. In the porch stood a woman looking anxiously from her husband on the seat to Auka with the hammer. There were many little children around her, clutching her skirts and peeking shyly at Auka from behind her. She was holding a baby, but to Auka all the other children looked about the same size. The woman looked at her husband. 'It's that bad, is it?' she said shrilly.

The tin man nodded. 'It means a new one this time, Afke. There's nothing else for it.'

'Did you make enough for a new one?'

The tin man winced. 'A bad week . . . Did you manage to keep anything over from last week?' he said timidly. His face flushed.

'Over?' she said. 'Over from last week?' She made a sweeping motion toward the children around her. 'And Janie had to have the doctor.'

Even the children looked sad and unhappy. They looked as if they understood such things. It was clear enough that the tin man couldn't buy a new wheel. It made Auka feel sad and helpless and unhappy for the tin man, for the wife, for all the children, and for himself—for it also meant no wheel for the school.

'Could the cooper fix it for you?' Auka suggested helpfully. 'He puts hoops around barrels and things; maybe he could make the rim stay on.'

The tin man and his wife looked startled. All the children stared big-eyed. 'Well, that's a new one,' the tin man said. 'That's one thing I haven't tried yet. I've had it at the blacksmith off and on, but I can't take it there again without money. The cooper,' he repeated, considering, 'that shouldn't cost too much.' He looked at his wife.

'I hope not,' she said softly. 'Otherwise maybe we'd better just pray. That's still free.' She looked defiantly at Auka.

'I'd better go now,' Auka said awkwardly. He did not know what else to say or what else to do. He handed the tin man his hammer but did not look at him. It was all so sad and hopeless; it made Auka feel full of lumps and unhappiness. And there wasn't a thing he could do.

'Thanks for helping,' the tin man said. 'And I only wish I could give you the wheel.'

'Oh, that's all right,' Auka said. 'It was sort of fun . . .' But that wasn't the right thing to say! 'In a way,' he added clumsily. Then he turned on his heels and ran.

It was such a relief to run away from the unhappiness that Auka ran harder and harder. The storks stopped him. There the two storks were again on the same house they had passed with the wagon. Both of them were coming down now with reeds in their bills —big as life—flapping low now, settling on the wheel on the roof, huge, white, wonderful—big as life. Auka stood staring up at them openmouthed.

Eyes on the storks, head thrown back, all absorbed, Auka edged into the little yard alongside the house. Now the storks were right above him on the roof. He felt almost as if he could reach up and touch them. A poorly placed twig fell from the great sprawly nest on the wagon wheel, rattled down the roof, and landed at Auka's feet. Auka picked it up and drew his arm back to toss it up to the storks. A woman rapped sharply on the windowpane. Auka dropped his hand. The woman shoved the window open. 'What are you doing in my yard?' she demanded. 'Who gave you permission?'

Auka brought his eyes down from the storks and became aware of the stick he was still holding. 'Oh,' he confusedly explained, 'they just dropped this down the roof, and I was going to toss it back.' He dropped the stick.

'You're a stranger here, aren't you?' the woman said. 'Do you always walk right into people's yards?'

'Oh, no!' Auka said. 'But there were the storks . . . I did walk right in here, didn't I?'

'Yes, and you must have unlatched the gate to do it.'

Auka managed an apologetic laugh. 'I suppose I did, but I didn't know it. You see, there were the storks so close, and in Shora we don't have storks at all. And you have them on your roof!'

The woman smiled at Auka's excited interest in her storks. 'Well, they're on the roof every year, and I guess one gets sort of used to them. Still, if you've never had a stork in your village, I suppose it is exciting.'

'Every year,' Auka said, wonder in his voice. 'And in Shora . . . Say!' he said suddenly. 'Are you maybe Lina's aunt? I go to school with Lina, and she wrote a story about what you told her about storks, and now we're all trying to find a wheel to put on our school to make storks come to Shora. That's why I'm away out here in Nes.'

'Well, now think of that!' the woman said. 'And Lina started it all? But, boy, I'm afraid it'll do no good to look for a wheel in Nes. Every spare wheel in Nes goes up on the roof every spring. Why, it's almost part of spring house-cleaning. You just noticed mine, because mine already has storks. I always get the first storks in Nes. But nearly every house has a wheel on the roof, as you can see. In fact, they're all up, except the one across the street. Evert is getting that up today, at least I see he's got the ladder up against the house. But Evert is always late—he's too fussy. He even *paints* his wheel.'

She stuck her head out of the window to look at the house across the street. Auka followed her gaze. An oldish man was coming around the house, rolling a wheel toward the ladder. 'Look at that!' Lina's aunt exclaimed scornfully. 'He's even gone patriotic this year and painted it red, white, and blue! At least other years he had it just one colour, and even then he never got a stork. Storks don't like all that bright colour. It scares them away. But you can't tell Evert anything, the stubborn old fool!'

Across the street the old man had begun to shove the wheel up the ladder. It was a big, heavy-looking, solid wheel, and Evert was having a struggle. The sheer weight of the wheel seemed to make it hard for him to get his foot on the next higher rung of the ladder.

'He'll never make it,' Auka said to Lina's aunt. 'Maybe I'd better give him a hand.'

Old Evert had stopped halfway up the ladder to rest. Now he stared up at the length of ladder and the steep pitch of roof still ahead of him. He looked around helplessly. His eyes fell on Auka. 'Hey, boy,' he yelled. 'Want to earn two and a half cents helping me get this wheel on the roof?'

'Sure,' Auka said promptly. Such money was not

just to be picked up every day, and he'd been going to do it for nothing! 'Bye, Lina's aunt,' he said hastily and hurried to the street. He remembered to close the gate.

'You can tell the old fool for me,' Lina's aunt said softly, 'he's wasting his money and his strength. Storks won't settle on a wheel that's lit up like a lighthouse.'

Auka didn't intend to say anything that might make him lose the surprise offer of two and a half cents. He sprinted across the street. 'What do you want me to do?' he asked Evert from the foot of the ladder.

'Get the other ladder that's behind the house and set it up next to mine. Then we can both push the wheel up. You can handle a ladder, can't you?'

For two and a half cents, Auka would have been willing to try to handle two and a half ladders. He hustled. He struggled the ladder up against the house, slid it tightly against Evert's ladder, then he climbed up and took hold of the wheel. 'That helps,' Evert breathed gratefully as he felt the strain ease. 'Once we get it on the edge of the roof we'll be all right.'

Auka looked at the heavy, solid wheel, looked up the long pitch of the tile roof, looked back at the solid wheel again, and then it struck him. 'What a work for nothing,' he said.

'What do you mean for nothing? I'm paying you, ain't I?'

'*You're* doing it for nothing!' Auka said pointedly. 'Lina's aunt says that you'll never get storks on a wheel that's painted red, white, and blue like a flag on a lighthouse. And she ought to know! The storks are already nesting on her wheel.' He nodded toward the roof across the street.

Evert looked at the roof across the street. With enormous flappings of its huge wings, a stork, with a twig crosswise in its bill, was just then settling down on the rim of the wheel.

87

'See that?' Auka said.

'Sure, I see it,' Evert said testily. 'But they'll land on mine just as well, once we get it up.'

'The bright paint will keep them away,' Auka said knowingly. 'What you need,' he pursued relentlessly, 'is an old wreck of a wheel—as long as it'll hold storks. Lina's aunt's is just an old wheel.'

'Oh, so,' Evert said. 'Well, all I've got is a good, solid, painted wheel, and they'll take it or leave it.'

'They'll leave it,' Auka said promptly, 'and next autumn you'll just have to haul it down again. What a work!'

'I called you over here to help me, not to give me an argument,' Evert said sourly. 'And if I didn't have to stand here arguing and holding up a heavy wheel at the same time, I'd give you a good sound swat around the ears!'

'No, but,' Auka said, 'I mean, I know where you can get just the wheel you need, good and old, and it doesn't have one speck of paint on it. It's even more of a wreck than Lina's aunt's.'

He put his shoulder under the wheel and took most of its weight, so he could carefully explain to Evert about the tin man and his hopeless wheel. 'He can't go out with it again,' Auka finished in all earnestness, 'no matter how long he soaks it in the canal.'

The man looked at him oddly. 'Well, you're a funny kid, bothering your head about other people's troubles. The tin man has always had troubles and always will with that houseful of kids. But those are his troubles, not yours nor mine.'

'No, but,' Auka persisted, 'if he had your wheel, he could use his wagon, and if you had his, you'd get storks.'

Evert looked at him hard. 'Boy, are you sure Lina's aunt isn't your aunt? You worry so about other people's business, you must be related.'

88

Auka stubbornly tried a new tack. 'Tomorrow is Sunday. If you don't get your wheel up today, you won't get at it again until Monday, and you're very late as it is. Lina's aunt's storks are already nesting.'

'Meaning what?' Evert demanded.

'I don't think I'll help you get it up,' Auka said determinedly.

'Then you don't get your two and a half cents.'

'No, but you won't get your storks. You won't anyway on a painted wheel, but . . .'

'Oh, all right!' Evert said. 'You're the most persistent, queer kid I've ever seen. But it's less work to give in to you than to stand on a ladder, holding a wheel, and arguing with you. Help me slide it down!'

Auka grabbed the wheel. When they had it resting against the foot of the ladder, he kept an eye on the man, expecting to get a hard box on the ear at any moment.

Evert grumbled to himself. 'A perfectly sound wheel for an old rotten thing,' he muttered, 'but then the tin man wouldn't have a red cent to pay me to boot.' He came to a decision. 'All right,' he said to Auka, 'roll it away and come back with the other. I'll give it a try. She across the street isn't going to rub my nose in it every year and every year again. Beat it!'

Auka jumped to take the wheel. 'I'll be right back, and then I'll help you put the old wheel up. It'll be much lighter. You'll see you'll get storks, and storks bring all kinds of good luck,' he promised in grateful excitement.

'Well, they're bringing the tin man some,' Evert said. 'Beat it before I change my mind.'

Auka rolled the wheel away. As he came down the street, Auka saw that the tin man, his wife, and all the little children were still around the wagon. The tin man was working on the old wheel. Auka couldn't wait. 'Look what I've got!' he yelled down the street.

89

He rolled the wheel wildly toward the astonished group around the wagon.

'We've got to get your old one off the axle right away, and then I've got to take it to Evert up the street,' he explained. 'We'd better work fast.'

'Evert?' The tin man couldn't believe it. 'Evert must be getting soft in the head,' he told his wife. They stood there awed by the glazed red, white, and blue wheel.

'I can explain while we change the wheel,' Auka said. 'We'd better do it quick—Evert might change his mind.'

Now the tin man sprang into action, and with Auka jabbering excitedly beside him, he soon had the wagon jacked up.

The old wheel had been off the axle so often, it practically fell off the moment the big nut that held it in place had been removed. Auka and the tin man slid the new wheel on the axle. The tin man had to step back a moment to admire the wheel. Auka twisted the nut into place and gave it a last hard turn with the wagon wrench. The tin man wasn't satisfied but had to give it another turn. Then he stepped back again.

With the new wheel in place, he at last seemed to be able to begin to believe his good luck. He rushed to the old wheel and heaved it on the wagon. 'Everybody on the wagon,' he shouted. 'All you kids, every single one. We're going to take this boy back to Shora in state on the wagon. You get on the wagon and catch them as I toss them up to you,' he excitedly ordered Auka.

Auka caught children as they came up to him and deposited them around his feet among the tin in the bottom of the wagon. Even the tin man's wife had to climb up on the high seat with the baby and share in the ride of triumph.

'We'll first ride up to Evert's to thank him and help

him get the old wheel on the roof. Then on to Shora,' the tin man said. 'Here's hoping Evert gets some storks on the old wheel. He's never had one. But I'll get him some storks if I have to catch them and tie them to Evert's wheel,' he promised. Everybody laughed happily at his excitement.

The wagon rattled and clattered and jangled to Evert's house. In all the excited talk of the thankful tin man, Evert wasn't given much chance to change his mind or even to think. With Evert watching in the confusion, Auka and the tin man swarmed up the ladders with the wheel. Even the steep roof seemed no problem to the tin man. He could have climbed walls and walked on clouds. In no time at all, the wheel was fastened to the brackets on the ridge of the roof.

'There now, Evert,' the tin man shouted down jubilantly, 'if the good Lord doesn't send you a couple of storks for such a good deed—as He will—I'll get them for you in person.'

'Tin ones?' Evert said sourly.

'No, good, lucky, live ones. Just like those.' He pointed to the nest on Lina's aunt's house. 'You'll see. You'll see. I . . .' Suddenly he was staring up into the sky. He pointed. 'There they come! There they come now. Get me down from here. Get the ladders down. Here come Evert's storks!'

Because he was so sure, everybody believed him. They hardly gave him time to scramble down the ladder. Even the tin man's wife helped to pull the ladders down, and they hastily laid them on the ground. Two of the children who had climbed out of the wagon were tossed back in again. The wife wasn't given time to get into the high seat. 'Just run alongside for a minute. I've got to get all this shiny tin away from Evert's house. It mustn't scare the storks,' the tin man said from his seat.

Auka and the wife trotted beside the wagon. Six houses beyond Evert's the wagon stopped. The tin man's wife got up into the high seat. Auka handed her the baby and climbed up after her. The tin man's eyes were fixed on the sky. In the wagon box the little children stared solemnly into the sky.

'Got to get this wagon still farther away,' the tin man muttered. 'All this shiny, jangling tin!'

They rattled farther down the street. Everybody stared up at the two flying storks. The storks were circling high over Nes. Back at the house Evert was crouched behind a bush, straining up, not moving a hair. The circling storks dipped lower and then still lower.

'I'd hate myself,' the tin man muttered, 'if I scared those storks away.' He clucked frantically to the horse. The old horse sensed the urgency in his voice. The wagon rattled out of Nes and on to Shora.

CHAPTER VIII

Lina and
the Upturned Boat

THE third little side road that Lina went down was the worst. She had gone singing down the other two lanes to let the people, and especially the watchdogs, know that someone was approaching. Luckily there had been someone at each house to hush the awful growlings of the watchdogs.

The people on these back farms had seemed only too pleased to have a young girl come visiting them. They had exclaimed and clucked sympathetically when Lina explained the wagon-wheel-on-the-school-for-storks project. Everybody had thought it the nicest idea. 'Shora lies so bare and naked against its dike,' one woman had said. 'It could well stand some storks to warm it up.' But nobody had had a wheel to spare. 'But, dearie,' the woman had said, 'if we had a spare wheel, you could be sure it would be on our own lonely roof. Every day I see the storks flying over, I wish I had a wheel. It's so quiet here, and storks are such company.'

The third little road seemed to have only one farm-house which was at its very end. There didn't seem to be a soul around. Nothing stirred in the farmyard

93

except some chickens and a goose under a wagon. Lina wished now she'd first run to the dike before going down this road. She wished she'd come singing, but she'd been thinking about what all the nice people had said on the farms on the other two roads. Here in the awful silence was nothing but a goose and some chickens under a wagon at the end of a short drive that led into the farmyard.

Lina took one step into the lane. Up in the wagon rose an enormous dog. All of a sudden there he stood, growling and barking—with the growls running under the quick, short barks—the growling never stopping.

Lina stood frozen where she'd stopped. The deep growling seemed to run along the ground at her. Her spine turned cold. She couldn't see whether the dog was tied in the wagon. What if he'd come in one leap from the wagon? What then? Nothing stirred, not a thing.

Lina did not know what to do. If she turned and ran, as all her quaking body wanted to do, the dog might come tearing after her. Now at least he only watched her with hard eyes and warned her away with his awful hoarse growling. A desperate plan came to Lina. She began singing at the dog—she didn't know what else to do. It came out queer and quavery, but she sang. She forced herself to sing louder. It had to sound as if she were coming on. She sang at the dog with all her might.

The surprised dog stayed on the wagon, but his ears flew erect at the shrill sound of the words that Lina sang at him. His growling had stopped. He uttered one bewildered bark then stood and stared in confusion, his ears pricked high.

It encouraged Lina. She sang and sang, and as she sang, she backed away. Any old song, any words—the dog couldn't know if they were right or wrong. She didn't herself. Then at last a hedgerow along the road hid the dog from sight for a moment. Lina turned and fled.

She kept singing wildly and looking over her shoulder. The dog was not following her. For all that, Lina shouted her song all the way back to the dike and up the dike. On the high dike she felt safe. She dropped in a panting heap on top of the dike. Now across the fields she could see the dog. He was still on the wagon. He had not moved except to turn his body from the lane toward the dike. His hard eyes still seemed to look at her. Lina shuddered.

Lina knew she could never nerve herself to go down another lane to another farmhouse—never. Her throat felt scratchy and raw from her hard singing. She never wanted to sing that song again either, whatever it had been. All she knew was that she felt sweetly safe here on the dike. Nothing could take you by surprise; you could see anything coming. She looked away from the dog and out over the quiet sea behind the dike. The tide was out; the water shimmered in the far distance, but below the dike the sea bottom stretched hard and dry in the ebb tide.

With loud, alarmed squawks a heron flew up from the dry sea. It fluttered awkwardly then came to rest on an old, upturned boat lying far out from the dike. The heron stood silhouetted against the high blue sky and the faraway blue of the water. It preened its feathers.

A heron wasn't a stork, but Lina stared fascinated at the lone bird on the lonely, forsaken boat. Teacher had said to look where a wheel couldn't possibly be. Well, a wheel couldn't possibly be in a boat—especially not under a stranded, overturned boat that had been lying there upside down for years. It had been lying there as long as—as long as history. A boat must certainly be the last place for a wagon wheel, but in

such places, teacher had said, the unexpected could
happen, could come up to surprise you. And there
were no dogs in the sea.

Slowly Lina crossed the dry strand, skirting the few
puddles left in hollow places from the last flood tide.
Even as quietly as Lina came, the heron heard her.
With a loud, disagreeable squawk it flapped up and
flew away over the dike. Lina was alone in the silent
dry stretches of the mysterious sea. Before her loomed
the dark old boat.

It was difficult to know how to climb to the top
of the high, round-bottomed fishing boat. Why she
wanted to get on the boat, Lina didn't exactly know;
except that now she was here, it seemed she had to do
something. She couldn't just walk around it and walk
back to sit on the dike! The whole boat looked slippery and slimy with seaweeds and sea scum. It was
crusted all over with strange rotted growths. Big crabs
scurried under the boat. It was so still here Lina could
hear the scuttling, clicking movements of the hard-

shell crabs. Snails and other slow slimy sea animals clung and moved everywhere among the weeds and rotted wood.

Lina walked around the boat once again. There was only one way to get up on it. An old anchor chain still hung at the stern. It was as coated and slimy as all the rest. If she clung to the chain and pulled herself up by it, she could sort of walk up the rounded stern—if she took her wooden shoes off.

Lina considered. She really should take her socks and stockings off, too, but the thought of climbing the crusted boat, with her bare toes among the slime and scum and moving things, gave her cold horror. She'd just take her shoes off. But when she set her shoes on the dry sea bottom, they looked so tiny and helpless and out of place in the big sea that Lina felt wretched. She couldn't leave them behind.

On sudden impulse Lina pulled the ribbon out of her hair, strung it through two holes in the sides of her wooden shoes, and hung the shoes around her neck by the ribbon. Then shutting her eyes tight, she grabbed the coated chain and, bracing her feet flat against the stern of the boat, hoisted herself up. It was far easier than she had expected.

Lina was on the boat. She stood surprised and pleased. She looked about her proudly, wishing that somebody could have seen her. Jella thought only boys could climb and jump. If it wasn't for skirts and dresses, she thought she could outclimb big heavy Jella any old day.

Oh, but it was quiet here! She wished now the heron had stayed. Lina hurriedly undid the ribbon from her shoes and put them back on. She left the ribbon around her neck; her hands were too dirty for her to put the ribbon back in her hair. She immediately felt much better with her shoes on. She moved carefully forward, feeling her way over the slippery boat bottom among the tiny scurrying animal-insect things.

There was a hole in the boat! A square hole had been cut into the bottom of the upside-down boat! But whatever for? Lina edged carefully toward the yawning hole, dropped to her knees, and queasily peered down. There was utter darkness and silence below except for the small faint sounds of crab scuttlings.

Gradually Lina's eyes became used to the darkness. Suddenly she thrust herself deep into the hole—head and shoulders—her eyes trying to pierce the darkness, trying to make sure. It wasn't, it couldn't be! It *was* a wheel!

Lina pulled her head out of the hole and glanced about her, blinking in the sunlight. Her mouth went partly open as if to shout the news to someone. But there was no one, and now in the stillness and sunlight she couldn't believe it herself any more. She must have imagined it in the darkness. Once more she plunged head and shoulders into the hole and hung down as far as she dared. It was so! It *was* a wheel! It was all but swallowed up in sea silt, but she could see part of a spoke, a little section of rim, and the big hub jutting up out of the silt.

A wagon wheel was under an old, forgotten, turned-up boat! It couldn't be, but it was!

Lina jumped to her feet. She danced a little dance all around the hole, forgetful of slime and slipperiness. She sang a little song in the stillness of sea. Danced and sang. It seemed to be the same song she had sung to the watchdog. It still had no meaning, it still made no sense, but now it was happy.

The song stopped abruptly in Lina's mouth; she stood still. Someone was watching her from the dike! It was old Douwa, and this was Douwa's boat, Lina knew. But she hardly knew old Douwa. Douwa lived in Shora, but you seldom saw him, because every day old Douwa took long walks along the dike—as far even as the village of Ternaad. It took him all day, but the next day he would do it over again. Old Douwa was ninety-three.

Now Douwa was shouting at her from the dike, but Lina on the boat couldn't understand his hoarse old voice.

'What did you say?' Lina called across the dry stretch of sea bottom.

And then each word came slowly to her. Douwa was shouting them one by one, 'Little girl, why were you dancing on my boat?'

'I found a wheel! I found a wheel!' Lina cried back at him.

'Oh, sure, but that's been there some eighty years.'

It overwhelmed Lina. She had to sit down. Imagine it! And Douwa had shouted it as if it were the most natural thing in the world. A wheel in a boat for eighty years and all the time old Douwa had known. And all the time through the search by the whole school, anyone could have gone up to him and said, 'Douwa, where can I find a wheel?' And he would have replied, 'Oh, under my boat.'

But who would have thought of asking Douwa? Douwa was almost a hundred years old.

A thousand questions seemed to bubble up in Lina. A thousand things she absolutely had to know about the wheel in the boat and about the hole. Why had they cut a hole in a boat? And everything and every amazing thing. Lina jumped to her feet. But you couldn't shout questions across such a distance. In her excitement, with her eyes fixed on Douwa and tingling to know, Lina ran down the rounded side of the boat and jumped to the packed sea bottom. She landed hard on hands and feet. One wooden shoe had made a splitting sound, but there was no time to think about that now. Lina picked herself up and raced across the

99

sea bottom to the dike. But when at last she stood before old Douwa on the dike, she was too breathless for questions.

'Just why,' the old man wanted to know, 'would a little girl be dancing on top of a boat because of a wagon wheel?'

Fortunately he now noticed Lina's split shoe. It gave Lina a chance to catch her breath. 'Better carry that shoe in your hand,' Douwa said. 'We'll go to my house and I'll staple a little fine wire over the vamp. It'll be good as new—if you don't jump from boats. But why were you doing that little dance there? You've got me as curious and inquisitive as old Grandmother Sibble.'

When Lina had her breath back, she explained why they wanted a wheel in Shora. She hurried to get it over so that she could ask Douwa why there was a wheel under a boat and why it seemed the most natural thing to him—when really it was a miracle and a wonder.

'So you need that wheel for storks,' Douwa said. 'Well, well, well . . .'

'But that square hole isn't nearly big enough to pull the wheel through,' Lina told him.

'No, of course not,' Douwa said. 'I cut it just big enough to pull a man through and not an inch bigger —not an inch.'

'A man?'

'My father,' Douwa said. 'And that was my father's wagon wheel you saw. It saved his life.'

'But, Douwa!' Lina exploded.

But old Douwa shook his head and pointed out to sea. A group of storks came winging out from sea, from far away near the islands. For a while they headed straight for Shora, straight toward Douwa and Lina, but near the old boat they swerved and flapped rapidly out of sight in the direction of Nes.

'There must have been twenty,' Lina said awed.

'No, exactly twelve,' Douwa said. 'But that isn't the point. If the storks are flying in flocks now and that wheel's got to be got out of the boat, we can't stand here talking. Tomorrow's Sunday, so there are no days to waste. The tide is soon due in from the sea, so there are no hours to waste. Besides all that, there's a storm brewing far back of the islands.'

Lina looked all around at the sunshiny blue sky over the distant blue sea then looked back at the old man in complete unbelief.

'Oh yes, that storm's coming,' Douwa said. 'Oh, it isn't a matter of hours; it won't come in a minute. But it's going to be such a storm that the tide won't leave the dike again for days on end. So this is our last chance to get near the boat. You see, little girl, we've no time to waste, and we'd better talk as we walk.'

'But where are we going? What will we do?' Lina said anxiously.

'We'll do what I did before, over eighty years ago. We'll go to my house to get my saw—and it's the same saw I used to cut my father out—then we'll hurry back and cut the hole big enough to pull the wheel out.'

Old Douwa, aided by his stout stick, strode along the dike so fast that Lina, hobbling on one shoe, had all she could do to keep up with him. She stumbled along in a daze, bewildered and seething with more and more questions. Lina looked eagerly up at the old man a few times, then she burst out with it. 'Douwa, I've got to know why there was a wheel in a boat, or I'll—I'll explode!'

Douwa grinned. 'That's easy,' he said calmly, never slackening his long stride. 'You see, my father was a fisherman, just like I was, and just as his father was before him. But all his life he was plagued by seasickness. He'd be sick all the weeks out on the sea and

101

until he got back home again. He hated the sea, but it brought him his living. He was a fisherman, like his father before him, so what could he do? Grub on the land? No, but do you know what he did? He put that wagon wheel on his boat. What belongs more with the solid, steady land than a wagon wheel? Nothing! It's reasonable, isn't it?'

'Yes,' Lina said in a small voice, picturing the sea-sick man, seasick all his life. 'Oh, yes! But then how did the wagon wheel save him?'

'There was the big storm. The fishing fleet didn't come back. It was a swift storm. It fell down on the fleet, and there was no running away from it or out before it. Not a boat came back. I was a little boy then in Shora. A week after the storm the tides brought in my father's boat—the only boat from the Shora fleet that ever came back. But it came back upside down. It stranded just about where it's lying now. Nothing could have lived in an overturned boat through such a week-long storm. The whole village was in sorrow; not a fisherman had come back. And there lay the boat —like a big tomb. Nobody went near it. I was a little boy, about as old as you are now. I used to go out on the dike and stare at the boat and cry all by myself. Every day—a little helpless, lonely boy.

'One day I got queer thoughts. I began dreaming things, imagining things, because it was too awful just staring at the boat that had been my father's tomb. I made up a story for myself. That my father was still in the boat, under the boat, but alive! It wasn't his tomb! Oh, it was foolish and wild, but it was so lonely when I cried there every day. Oh, it was impossible . . .'

'But it was so, wasn't it?' Lina said urgently. 'Because it was so impossibly impossible, it was so!'

The old man looked at her. 'Precisely,' he said, as if he were talking to a grown-up. 'Impossibly impossible —but exactly!' he said. 'Little girl, how did you ever think of it? That's the way I wish I could have explained it, because that's the way I thought it as a child. But I had no words.'

'Our teacher told us,' Lina started to explain, but the old man was not listening.

'I went out to the boat,' he said softly. 'The tide was out; the boat lay high. And there I stood beside the looming boat in the quiet sea, and I was scared, because this was my father's boat, and my father was gone. I couldn't believe my dreams out there in the sea. But just the same I laid my ear against the side of the boat, and I listened a long time. I thought I heard a faint tapping. Oh, hardly louder than the noises of the hard-shell crabs. Then I was sure. And I yelled. "Dad, Dad," I screamed. "Just wait, I'm coming back. Dad, I'm coming back to get you." As if he hadn't been waiting there for days.

'I think I kept yelling and screaming, in between crying, all the way to Shora. I yelled down the street. Nobody would believe me. And my poor mother said, "No, Douwa, no. Your father is gone. Hush, boy."

'Oh, I couldn't stop to explain. Everybody thought I was crazy. You don't know the awful, dreadful hurry. I grabbed an axe and a saw. I ran all the way back, alone. I was little, but I was strong and I was excited. I chopped a hole in the bottom of the overturned boat, and when it was big enough to push a saw through, I sawed and sawed. And every once in a while I'd have to stop and yell, "Dad, Dad," through the hole. And he answered me in a weak whisper of a voice. And then I'd saw like a maniac again.

'At last the hole was cut, and I could push myself in. There was my father right below me, there on the wheel. The wheel was leaning against the side of the boat. With his last strength my father had climbed to the hub to be as close to me as possible while I sawed, to be within reach. I leaned in; I grabbed

103

him under the arms; I lifted him out. I was small, but I was strong. Right then I could have lifted the church and the tower. Too, my father was just a light skeleton.'

Lina was crying a little as she hobbled beside the old man. He was striding so fast in his excitement of living it all over again, he was almost running. It was sweet to cry about it a little, because it had happened more than eighty years ago and was a miracle and a wonder.

'Know how he lived under that boat all those days?' the old man almost shouted. 'By climbing to the top of the wheel whenever the tide came in so as to keep his head above water. The boat hadn't mired so deep in the sea silt then; the tide didn't flow over it the way it does now. Know what he ate? Candles! Pieces of candle, that they'd had in the boat, came floating around him in the flood tides. Know what he drank? Fish and crabs. He'd chew the juices out of them for a little water and spit the salty raw flesh out again. But he was a skeleton.

'And there I stood on top of that boat, a boy with his father—I was almost crazy with excitement. And then, just the way you did, I ran down the side of the boat carrying my father. We landed in a heap, but I picked him up. I ran with him over the dry sea bottom and over the dike to Shora. I kicked the door open, and I yelled, "Mum, here's my dad." And my mother fainted. What a day! What a great day!'

Together they strode along the dike, and Lina looked up at the old man in wonder.

'Now I'm doing it again,' old Douwa said suddenly. 'Almost a century later, I'm doing it again. Running home for the same saw. I'm going to do it again. Cut a hole; this time for my father's wagon wheel. And it's going on the school! You know, little girl, that is wonderful and that is right. The wheel on

104

the school as a sort of monument to my father who was saved by that wheel.'

'Oh,' Lina gasped. 'Oh, yes, Douwa, yes!'

'But we're going to need help to lift that water-logged wheel out of the silt and up through the hole.'

'Won't it be rotten?' Lina asked anxiously. 'After almost a century?' It seemed such endless ages.

'It'll be as sound as the day it landed there. Under the water and in the moist silt, it would be almost eternal. Wood under salt water doesn't rot.'

'Then I'm going to run and tell the teacher,' Lina said. 'He'll ring the school bell, and all the boys will come. They can help us. But it'll take a while. They're all over the countryside.'

'Fine,' the old man said. 'I'll get the saw and a shovel. We can start making the hole bigger and dig the wheel out of the silt while they come in from the country. Tell your teacher everybody's to hurry. The tide will soon be in. Here, give me that wooden shoe, so I can fix it. No, better give me both, then you can run faster and get to that school.'

Lina hastily handed the old man both her wooden shoes and dashed off. Far behind her she could hear the old man's heavy stick pounding the brick in his fierce stride.

There was no one in the school. The teacher was gone. The door of the school stood wide open, but there was no one. Lina rushed into the classroom and stood puzzled in the empty room. But the teacher had said he'd be at school all day! Maybe *she'd* better ring the bell to make them all come. Lina darted to the porch where the bell rope hung. There was no bell rope! Lina stared bewilderedly around her. Then with a helpless shrug, she dashed out of the school and back to the village and old Douwa.

The whole village seemed deserted; the street lay empty; even Grandmother Sibble III wasn't sitting in her porch. Lina rushed on, looking everywhere. She came to a dead stop in the middle of the street. The gate to Janus's high-fenced back yard stood wide open! It was startling; it had never happened before. For a split second Lina considered dashing in there. Oh, but that was silly. Janus had no legs; he'd be useless. In desperation Lina ran right past Douwa's house to the dike to see if, from the high dike, she could find any of the boys or the teacher somewhere in the level, flat fields. There was nothing in all the fields except the stooping figures of farm workers.

Lina turned to look at the faraway upturned boat. There was old Douwa, striding out along the dike toward the boat, an axe and a shovel and a coil of rope thrown over his shoulder. He hurried along with his big stout stick. He was carrying her shoes in his other hand. Douwa hadn't even waited for her. On silent stockinged feet Lina ran after him along the top of the dike.

From a distance Jana, the wife of Janus, coming home with her yoke and empty breadbaskets, saw old Douwa rushing along the dike with a saw and shovel. Jana was far out along the road; she had been peddling bread to the outlying farms between Shora and Nes. Now there came Lina running hard after the old man! Jana set her baskets down in the middle of the road, rested her yoke, and stood and stared.

Old Douwa plunged down the sea side of the dike and disappeared from Jana's view. A distance behind him, Lina, too, ran down the dike and disappeared. Jana in a confused way stooped to pick up a few smooth stones from the gravel road and started to drop them in a basket. Suddenly she grabbed up her yoke and baskets and took off for Shora as fast as she could. Her billowing skirts fluttered.

Lina at last caught up with Douwa as he was nearing the old boat. 'Oh, you *can* walk,' she panted. 'I couldn't catch up, and I couldn't find anybody in Shora. Everybody's gone. Even the teacher. Now what will we do?'

'We'll do what we can, you and I. After that's done, we'll think what to do next. No sense worrying ahead.'

'But how will you get up on the boat?'

'How did you get up?' Douwa asked.

'I climbed up by the anchor chain at the stern.'

'Then I'll have to climb up the anchor chain at the stern, too.'

'But you're almost a hund—— You're ninety-three!'

'So I am, and that can't be helped. All I can do is try and climb.' The old man chuckled proudly at Lina's unbelieving look. 'Up you go first,' he said.

With a boost from Douwa, Lina climbed up easily. After handing her the long-handled shovel and throwing the saw and coil of rope up to her, old Douwa tossed up Lina's shoes for her to catch. Next he tossed her his own. 'Can't leave them down here in case the tide wants to come in,' he said. 'Hey, wait a minute. My stick!' He threw the stick up to Lina.

'And now we commence to climb!' he announced cheerfully. 'Let my rope down, because I'm afraid I'm going to need a little help.' He tied the rope around his chest. 'I sometimes overestimate myself, but with you pulling as hard as you can and me climbing as hard as I can, I believe we're going to make it.'

He grabbed the chain and, bracing his feet flat against the stern of the boat, started to come up. Halfway up he was breathing hard. 'Keep pulling,' he gasped. 'Pull harder.'

Lina tugged with fierce strength. The old man made a terrific scrambling effort, and up he came. For a moment he stood teetering on the end of the boat, but he steadied himself, took a step forward, and let out a long breath. 'You see,' he said, 'just between the two of us, and here I am.'

'Oh, Grandpa Douwa, you're wonderful!' Lina said.

'Don't you grandpa me!' the old man ordered. 'Grandpas sit in corners; they don't climb boats.'

But he had to sit down and rest a while. 'You've got breath,' he said. 'Start sawing.'

The wood was old, but it was thick. The inner core of the heavy planks was sound and solid oak. Lina sawed until she could no longer move her arm up and down. She looked at her sawing. She had sawed no more than an inch of the thick wood—if that! She looked at Douwa. The old man chuckled. 'You've got to learn to pace yourself. Steady does it, long strokes—not that jerky jiggling.'

He got to his feet and came over to the hole. 'Maybe I'd better saw and you dig, then we'll get two things done. You won't be scared down there in the dark with the crabs and things?'

'Not with you up here, and a wheel down there,' Lina said stoutly. 'But when we've got the hole sawed and the wheel dug free, then what? Can you and I get it out together?'

'No, we can't,' the old man said mildly, 'but I think I've taken care of that. I saw you come running after me alone. I reckoned you hadn't found anybody to help us, because I hadn't heard any school bell ring. So then when Jana, coming home from her bread peddling, saw me rushing along the dike with a saw and shovel, I purposely plunged down the dike and disappeared. By now Jana's rushed home to Shora to tell everybody old Douwa's gone clean out of his head.' He chuckled. 'You watch! It won't be long before the women will be coming out along the dike. They all baby me so.' He tied the rope around Lina's chest. 'But down with you now, and get that wheel

108

dug free before the tide comes sweeping in. Ready? Down you go.'

Jana dropped her yoke and breadbaskets in the street, ran up the steps of old Douwa's house, and stormed into the front room. 'Janka, Janka, are you there?' she yelled through the house.

There were stumbling noises in the kitchen. Janka, Douwa's granddaughter, came running. 'Is something wrong?'

'You've got to face it, Janka. It's finally come,' Jana told the woman sombrely. 'Your grandfather's mind has finally gone back on him. There he was running out along the dike with a saw and a shovel to get his father out again—and his old father dead and gone these sixty years.'

'Oh, no,' Janka said weakly. 'And only this morning we were talking about it—how sound Grandfather was staying in mind and body, and he going on ninety-four and walking to Ternaad every day.'

'Well, I saw him running out in the direction of the old boat with a saw and shovel.'

'But he was gone all day on his long walk. Where would he have got a saw and shovel? A saw! Wait a minute.' Janka dashed out of the room.

Jana left behind alone looked out of the window. She saw Lena, Lina's mother, evidently going to the shop—at least she had a shopping basket on her arm. Jana rushed out to the steps. 'Lena,' she called urgently. 'Lena, can you come a moment?'

Jana had put such mystery and calamity into her call that by the time Lina's mother reached the steps, all the women of Shora had been alerted. Curtains were pushed back in place behind windows, and in almost every porch appeared a woman. Some came with brooms to make it look as if they'd just innocently come out at that particular moment to sweep

their porches. Others leaned out and craned their necks honestly. Even Grandmother Sibble III had come out.

To everybody's relief Jana now began making motions for all the women to come. They bustled down the street. Unable to follow, Grandmother Sibble settled herself on her chair and sat rocking herself back and forth in inquisitive impatience. She held a forgotten piece of rock candy between thumb and forefinger.

The women reached the steps just as Janka, Douwa's granddaughter, burst out of the house. 'You're right, Jana,' Janka said hysterically. She was pale with fright. 'He did take the saw! The saw is gone! There it's hung over the fireplace all these years, but it's gone. He must have come in when I went to the shop.'

'What is it? What is this?' Lina's mother demanded.

'It's old Douwa gone out of his mind, Lena. And

your girl, Lina, was running after him,' Jana told her soberly. 'But what can that poor scrap do with a strong old man gone out of his mind?'

'He can be so stubborn,' Douwa's granddaughter said.

'And all the men out at sea!' one of the women exclaimed. Then with one accord, talking excitedly, the women set off for the dike.

'That's right,' one of the women suddenly remembered. 'There isn't a man in Shora. Not even the teacher and your Janus, Jana!'

Jana whirled on her. '*My* Janus?'

'Yes, left his yard and cherry tree. Left Shora with a rake—went with the teacher and four boys pushing him in the wheel chair.'

Jana wouldn't believe it for a moment. 'Not my Janus,' she said firmly. 'Boys pushing him? Hah, not my Janus!'

'Well, make me out as a liar, then,' the other retorted hotly. 'But I saw him. Why, I even called after him, "Janus, what's wrong? What's happened?" Do you know what he yelled at me over his shoulder as he flew by? "Nothing, woman, nothing's wrong. But I haven't had so much fun since that shark bit off my legs."'

'Shark bit off his legs?' Jana muttered, completely mystified. 'What is this? Is everybody going out of his mind?'

They passed Grandmother Sibble's house. 'What's happening?' Jana shouted at the old lady. 'You see everything going on in this village. What's happening in Shora, Grandmother Sibble?'

In their haste, none of the women could possibly wait for an answer, and Grandmother Sibble made no attempt to reply. She watched them rush off to the dike. She chuckled to herself. 'What's happening, Jana, is a wagon wheel for storks,' she said softly to herself. She rocked herself in delight and stuck the piece of candy in her mouth.

The women of Shora rushed up the dike steps, dreading what they might see on the other side.

On top of the dike the women stood in a row and stared into the distance where the old, upturned boat loomed. On the boat they could see the stooped figure of Douwa. He was kneeling and was sawing with all his might.

'But where's Lina?' Lina's mother demanded.

The women searched the empty strand, but there was no girl anywhere in sight in all the dry distance of the sea bottom. 'Oh, no!' a woman suddenly exclaimed. She pointed. 'Isn't that the tide coming in?'

Far away toward the islands and almost beyond their sight, a thin crawling silvery line was forming. 'There!' the pointing woman said urgently. 'Can't you see it? Over there, right over against the islands.'

'It is the tide!' Another woman saw it at last. 'The tide's coming. We've got to get Douwa down from that boat before he gets cut off from the dike. At high tide that whole boat goes under.'

They ran. They ran clumsily in their billowing, heavy skirts and wooden shoes. The tide was faster. The thin, innocent-looking silvery line, that had been so far away it could hardly be seen, came with a slithering snaky rush. Right on behind the ground tide rushed the deeper tide, deepening moment by moment until, far out at sea, a great wall of water formed itself and came roaring toward the land.

Old Douwa on the boat glanced briefly out to sea. 'Have you got that wheel dug free?' he shouted down the hole to Lina. 'The tide'll be here in a few minutes.'

'Almost,' Lina said. 'But it's so big and such a long way to dig around.' She dug frantically again.

Lina dug and the old man sawed. 'It's free,' Lina shouted up a moment later. She stopped for breath. 'I've been trying to set it up, but I can't even stir it, it's so heavy.'

As she was talking, the first hissing line of bottom water slid swiftly under the boat and curled coldly around her toes. Lina gasped. 'Oh, it's here,' she yelled. 'The water 's here.'

The old man stooped down to the hole. 'Can you climb a rope?'

'No,' Lina said promptly. 'I've tried lots of times, but dresses get in your way.'

'Well, take the dress off.'

There was a little silence. 'Oh, I don't know. Should I? Can't you pull me up?'

'Listen, tides take no time for modest little girls. That rope 's got to be tied to the wheel—how else are we going to pull it up out of there? Tie the rope to the wheel. I'll hold the rope taut, and you climb it. If we don't do it that way, we won't have a wheel.'

Again there was a silence. Then a small voice called, 'I've tied the rope around the wheel and my dress around my neck. I'm ready.'

The old man straddled the hole, stretching the rope tight while Lina climbed.

Now the women of Shora had gathered on the point of the dike opposite the old boat. The tide had kept them from getting to it and had driven them back to the dike. They stood shouting frantic words at Douwa across the distance, but the old man was too occupied with straining at the rope and holding it steady for Lina to answer.

As she climbed, Lina heard the women's sharp shrieks. Now her head came up through the hole. The old man reached down with one hand to grasp her, but Lina saw the women. 'My mother,' she gasped. 'And me with my dress off. Oh, will I catch it!'

'I'm standing in their way, and the moment I pull you out, I'll even turn my back,' old Douwa said. He grinned at her and lifted her out.

Behind the old man's broad back, Lina hastily unknotted the dress. 'All right now,' she whispered.

At the first sight of Lina, Lina's mother had rushed down the dike; she'd run into the water a little way toward the boat. The rushing ground swell of the tide sent the water up over her knees. Knee-deep in water she stood screaming, 'Lina! Lina, come now—or it will be too late!'

'Come down, come down,' the chorus of women screamed desperately from the dike. Now Douwa's granddaughter, Janka, rushed down into the sea after Lina's mother. 'Let yourself slide and run through the water, both of you,' she shrieked. 'You can still do it.'

'Get a farmer,' Douwa shouted back at her. 'Get a farmer to come with horse and wagon. That's all we need.'

He chuckled to himself when he saw the women on the dike turn and disappear over the crest of the dike to run to one of the farms around Shora. Only Lena and Janka, the mother and the granddaughter, still hovered beneath the dike. They stood close together, clutching each other in order to stay on their feet, but bit by bit the rising tide forced them back to the dike.

'Lina, Lina, it's away over our knees! It's your last chance now,' Lina's mother screamed.

'Are we going to stay here?' Lina asked Douwa desperately.

'Yep,' the old man said. He was calmly fishing his pipe from his pocket. 'What your mother doesn't realize is that if now it's over their knees there below the dike, it's over your head out here. But the old boat is high. It'll be easily an hour before the tide goes over the boat, so you and I will stay here high and dry until help comes. That's why I sent them for a horse and wagon—not only to get us two off but to get that waterlogged wheel to shore, too.' He chuckled as he filled his pipe and looked out to sea.

Lina paced back and forth on the boat.

'Now you'd better yell to your mother to get back on that dike before the real sweep of the tide knocks her off her feet. See, there it comes!' The old man pointed to the great wall of water rushing toward them from out the deep, distant sea. He began lighting his pipe.

'Mother, get back, get back!' Lina called across the rushing water. 'It's coming! Hurry, run up on the dike. We're all right here.'

Her mother and Janka plunged through the deepening water and scurried up the dike. But near the bottom of the dike, the two women whirled desperately. Once more a scream came across to the boat as the wall of water came thundering. 'What will we do? Oh, what will we do?'

'You'd better sit down here with me,' Douwa told Lina. 'Pacing back and forth on this slippery boat, you might slide off. Sitting is safer. Just let them scream; it makes them feel a little better. The others are getting a farmer, and that's all needs to be done. Even if the tide goes over the boat before the farmer gets here, we'll just get our feet wet. And since you're young and don't have to worry about rheumatism, when it comes that high, I'll just have to sit on your shoulders.'

Lina choked and gave the old man an astonished look. Then she laughed. His jokes and his calmness were beginning to quiet her. She sat down beside the old man and laid her hand in his. 'I never knew you were so funny,' she said gratefully. 'I didn't know people were funny when they were old.'

The old man was pleased. 'There, that's much better. No sense running up and down this boat like a headless chicken.'

115

But Lina had to stand up a moment. 'Mother, we're really all right up here,' she yelled as loud as she could. 'There's nothing to worry about, Douwa says. And, Mother, WE'VE GOT A WHEEL.'

She settled herself beside the old man. 'Isn't this exciting? We've got a wheel, and you and I got it. Mother, we're all right here!' she shouted suddenly. 'Douwa knows!' But this time she didn't get up to shout. 'She won't believe me, anyway,' she told the old man. She held his hand tightly as the wall of water, with a searing, cutting noise and then a thunderous roar, rushed threateningly deep along the old boat and on to the dike. Behind the wall of water, the sea surrounded the boat and lapped up against its rounded sides.

'Isn't this exciting?' Lina whispered. She clung to the old man.

CHAPTER IX

The Wheel Rim

WHEN the soaked Eelka and the dripping Jella
arrived in Shora, they hurried down the street to
bring their load of wheel spokes and rim sections to
the school. 'I don't know if anybody in Shora has a
rake, do you?' Eelka asked doubtfully. 'With no trees
and hardly any gardens, there's nothing to rake in
Shora.'

'The teacher might have one,' Jella said. 'He's got a
little garden.' The words stopped in his mouth, and he
nudged Eelka. There stood Pier and Dirk in the open
gateway of Janus's back yard, talking to Janus! 'Look
at that!' Jella said in an unbelieving whisper.

'Something's up,' Eelka said and hurried right into
Janus's yard. Now he, too, stood in the gateway, talking
and talking, explaining everything to Pier, Dirk, and
Janus. Jella stayed in the street. But Eelka mentioned
him to Janus. 'Jella, come on,' he yelled. 'Janus wants
to see those rim sections.'

117

Jella did not move.

Janus wheeled himself to the gate. 'Come on, kid. I don't bite.'

'No,' Jella said doubtfully, 'but you hit awfully hard.'

'Oh, that's right; you're the big kid I leathered last year,' Janus said. Out of the side of his mouth, he said to the three boys around him, 'Maybe I did do it a bit hard if he remembered it a whole year.'

With everybody looking at him, waiting for him, Jella had to come. He came, but over his loaded arm he kept warily looking at Janus and was ready to turn and run like a hare if he had to. Jella suspected some trap. It wasn't right, Janus sitting there talking to kids. Something must be going to break loose in a minute.

'Janus just wants to see if those pieces of rim can be fitted and glued together again,' Eelka explained reassuringly.

Jella stepped up, dumped the whole load of rim sections before Janus's chair, and hastily stepped back out of reach. Janus had made no attempt at all to grab him; instead he rummaged among the rim sections that Jella had put before him. He sorted and fitted, trying to fit the different pieces together the way they had been originally. The other boys stood absorbed. 'Is Janus going to fix it for us?' Jella whispered. He couldn't believe it.

Janus heard him 'It can be done,' he told Jella, 'but it'll take time. Some glue, a few screws, and some small nails. Storks aren't too fussy.'

'But it won't stay without an iron rim to hold it together, will it?' Jella asked. He forgot his fear now that it seemed there was a possibility the wheel could be put together again. He crowded in close between Dirk and Pier to see just what Janus was doing with the pieces. Janus dropped the sections he was holding so suddenly, Jella jumped back. But Janus just said, 'Right you are, kid. You've got something besides beef above your neck. This is wasting time. Come on, let's go and get that rim.'

'We'll need a long rake to drag the canal—the mud is so deep,' Eelka told him.

'A rake,' Janus considered. 'Now who in Shora would have a rake? They use that on land, don't they?'

It was a joke, but nobody but Pier seemed to feel enough at ease with Janus to laugh. Pier sniggered out loud, but when he saw he was laughing alone, he sobered and said, 'The teacher's got one, Janus. I know. I had to help him with his garden once—for punishment, instead of staying after school.'

'On to that teacher,' Janus commanded. 'Come on, let's go.' He grabbed the wheels at the side of his chair to propel himself. 'On to the school,' he bellowed. He seemed to be full of good spirits.

'I'll push you, Janus,' Pier offered.

'I will, too,' Dirk said.

Eelka hastily piled his spokes beside Jella's scattered rim sections and jumped to help with Janus's wheel chair. 'May I, Janus? Janus, may I push you?'

'Let's see . . .' Janus studied the four as if it were a deep problem. Then he pointed to Jella. 'You, big fellow, you push. Maybe if you do something for me, you won't be so scared of me.'

With Jella behind the chair, they started off down the street to the school. But the other three boys couldn't keep their hands off; the strange wheel chair was too fascinating. They started off sedately enough, but with all four pushing, Jella and Pier from behind, Dirk and Eelka at the sides, they were soon going at a half run. The wheel chair went bouncing and jouncing over the irregular street. Janus had to hang on with all his strength, but he seemed to like it. And since he didn't object, the boys went still faster—now

119

they were almost at a full run. 'Yippeeee!' Janus
yelled out ahead to the empty street. 'Out of the way,
all you mortals. Janus is coming.'

The boys shoved still harder.

'Boys, this is it. This is making the old wheel chair
go. It never knew it could go so fast.' Janus was quiet
a moment. 'Hey, Pier,' he yelled over his shoulder,
'this is almost as much excitement as when the shark
bit off my legs.'

Yelling and laughing, with the wheel chair rattling,
they arrived at the school. The teacher came running
from the classroom at the strange sounds outside. By
the time he reached the door, the boys had already
shoved Janus and the wheel chair into the school
porch. The teacher and Janus met each other full tilt.
It was almost a collision.

'Is something wrong?' the startled teacher asked.
'What's happened?'

'What's happened, Teacher, is that these kids found
a wheel but then promptly went and lost the rim in
the canal. But they say you own a rake, so we've come
to borrow it to drag the canal.'

'It fell apart,' Eelka explained. Then they were
all explaining together. The confused teacher finally
held up his hand. 'What I get out of this is that you
need a rake, so I'll get my rake from home. Then we'll
all go to the canal, and you can explain it all on the
way.'

He skirted the group and rushed out of the door.

'I think I like that man,' Janus observed. 'Never
had much to do with high-minded teachers since I was
a kid, but he means business. I thought teachers just
talked, but he doesn't fool around with the words. He
goes and does things.'

The boys wheeled Janus's chair around to push him
out of the porch again. At that moment Janus saw the
bell rope hanging in the porch. 'Hey, a rope!' he said.

'I should have thought of it. We need a rope. That bottom mud in the old canal goes so deep in places, we may have to tie a rope to the end of the rake.' He grabbed at it.

'Hey, don't!' Pier warned. 'That will ring the bell, and then everybody will come, because if the bell rings, that means a wheel has been found.'

'Well, a wheel has been found, hasn't it?' Janus said impatiently. 'At least nine-tenths of a wheel. But don't worry—if I yank that rope with a good enough snap, something will give without ringing the bell.' He reached up and gave the rope a tremendous snapping jerk. The rope parted somewhere above in the cupola and came tumbling down around Janus's head. 'There,' he said, 'now we've got a rope.' He proceeded calmly to coil it around his arm.

Janus just did things! He hadn't even asked the teacher's permission! The boys looked at him in awe and stared up at the empty hole in the porch ceiling through which the bell rope had always hung.

'No wonder you could hardly walk for a week,' Eelka whispered to Jella and tenderly rubbed the seat of his own pants as if feeling the pain.

The teacher appeared in the school doorway. He had the rake, but right away he missed the bell rope. He stared at the empty rope hole in the ceiling.

'Reckoned we might need a rope, too,' Janus explained.

'Oh, I see,' the teacher said faintly. 'Oh, yes.'

'Well, are we ready?' Janus asked. 'Then let's get going.' Outside he took the rake from the teacher and laid it across his lap. 'Seeing I'm riding,' he explained with a grin. 'And,' he added, 'you'd better tie this rope around my chest and the back of the chair so that I won't go flying out on my face, the way these crazy kids take me down the street.'

The teacher, following his instructions, wound the

rope tightly around Janus's chest and bound him to the back of the chair. 'Can you run?' Janus asked the teacher. 'Because we really move.'

The four boys giggled. A teacher was a dignified, important person, and Janus asked him to run!

To their amazement the teacher grinned. 'Well,' he said, 'I should be able to keep up with a wheel chair, and if I can't, you and I had better change places.'

Janus liked that! He bellowed a big laugh. 'You're all right!' he told the teacher approvingly. But the wheel chair was moving too sedately for him. He looked around. 'Well, you kids—what's the matter? Just because the teacher 's here, you'd think I was a delicate baby in a pram. Get going; get the lead out of your pants.'

With a doubtful look at their teacher, the boys shoved a little harder. When the teacher still made no objection, they increased the speed. Now they actually

had the teacher running beside the wheel chair at a half run, he still looked good-natured about it.

'Here we go!' Jella warned the others out of the side of his mouth. 'Look out, you mortals in Shora,' he yelled out in imitation of Janus.

Janus leaned eagerly forward against his rope—ready. The boys shoved him ahead with all their might. Now they tore down the Shora street at full speed. They went at such a pace that Dirk and Pier at the sides had all they could do to steady the bouncing, jumping wheel chair. But Janus was shouting things at some woman they passed. Just out of Shora, Eelka had to fall out; the pace was too much for him. But he couldn't stand being left either; he came trotting on behind.

All out of breath, except Janus, they arrived at the spot in the canal where the rim had gone down. Janus was all for starting to fish for the rim at once, but the teacher protested. 'Remember, we ran all the way.

Now we've got to do a little breathing,' he said. 'Wait till we catch our breaths. Mine's still back there in Shora.'

'Breathe all you like,' Janus said generously. 'I'll study the situation meanwhile.' He propelled himself and the wheel chair so close to the canal's edge that the alarmed teacher, who had sunk down in the grass, jumped up again to hold the chair back. Jella hurriedly grabbed one of the wheels; Dirk and Pier took the other. Now Eelka came puffing up; he, too, took hold of the wheel chair.

Unconcerned with all the stir and worry, Janus began dragging with the rake. With everybody hanging on to the chair, he leaned against the rope and reached out as far as he could. After his tenth cast with the rake, he began to look doubtful. 'That mud must be bottomless here. I don't know, Teacher, but it looks to me as if you'd better send a telegram to Australia: "Have you seen a wagon wheel rim down there?" '

None of the boys laughed. They stared sombrely into the canal. Eelka came up from behind the chair and peered along the canal. 'Hey, there's the hub out there, tight against the bank.' He pointed out the hub to Janus.

'You'll need the rake to get that out, too,' Janus said as he threw the rake out again.

At the very next cast the rake struck something hard. Janus worked furiously, probing the spot, trying to get the rake to take hold of whatever it had hit. 'Got it,' he said at last. But what the rake brought to the surface was only an old enamel pail full of mud. In his disgust Janus hauled it up by the end of the rake and flung it far. 'At least that's out of our way.' He turned to Eelka. 'Here, kid,' he said. 'You get that hub first. We've got to try something different.'

'Let me do it, Eelka,' the teacher said, taking the

rake. 'I've been feeling so useless here.' He hurried down the canal.

The boys pulled the chair back from the canal's edge. Janus prepared the rope. 'We'll try it with the rope tied to the rake as soon as he gets back. We're going to have to go really deep. And if that rope is long enough, I'm going to get that rim out. Ought to find it with the rake on the end of a rope. Going to find it. Man, I haven't had so much fun since that shark bit off my legs!' He looked blandly at Dirk and Pier.

Jella's mouth fell open. Eelka stared at Janus. 'Both legs in just one bite?' he asked in awe.

Janus shrugged. 'Am I supposed to know how many bites?' he asked. 'I wasn't looking around just then.'

'What did you do?' Jella said.

'I kicked his teeth out, that's what I did!'

Pier was enjoying the solemn awe of Jella and Eelka; he couldn't resist! 'But he'd bitten off both your legs, you said,' he pointed out to Janus.

'Did I say both at one time?' Janus said and glared fiercely at Pier. 'He was still sawing away on one tough old sea boot. So I kicked him in the teeth with the other. That's where I made my mistake. It made him so mad, he just bit off the other. Then I couldn't kick him again, having no more legs left.'

'I hope those sea boots gave that shark a stomach-ache, worse than green cherries,' Pier said, looking solemnly around at all the others.

'Me, too,' Jella said fervently.

Eelka stood dithering, mouthing a question he badly wanted to ask Janus about the shark. But Janus saw the teacher coming back with the hub. At once he had to be pushed back to the canal and became too busy for questions. He tied the rope to the rake handle, threw the rake far out into the canal, and let it sink. Slowly he dragged in the rope. Suddenly the

125

rake caught. 'Now then,' Janus said, 'hang on to the chair. That's the rim, and now it's coming up here to me or my name isn't Janus.' His enormous arms swelled and quivered with the strain. He began to draw the rope and rake and whatever load hung on it toward the canal bank. It was such a tug that the cords in his straining neck swelled and his arms bulged.

Suddenly something snapped. They had all been straining so hard to hold the wheel chair back, they jerked Janus and the chair far back from the bank before they could regain their balance. The rake handle, still tied to the rope in Janus's hands, floated on the surface of the water. 'Well, there went Shora's only rake,' Janus said gloomily. No one else said a word. All stared in dismay at the rake handle in the canal. 'Well, now we're just going to have to think out something else,' Janus said. He sounded almost too cheerful about it. 'Let's get back to Shora. I'll rig up something, some way.'

No one said a word. In the heavy silence Janus jerked his head up. 'Did you hear that?' He held his hand up for silence. It came again, the sound that only Janus had heard. The wind brought it along the canal. It sounded like screaming, like women screaming. It sounded as if the wind was bringing it from the dike at the far side of the village. Again the wind picked up the sound. It whisked by their ears along the quiet canal.

Janus grabbed the wheels of his chair and whirled the chair around. 'Those are women. Something's wrong.' His eyes shot to the weather vane on top of the tower and then to the sun in a quick estimate of time and wind direction. 'Ah,' he said, 'the tide's in. Most likely some sheep strayed down the dike and got themselves flooded in the tide and now are standing there just like sheep, letting themselves drown. Let's go. We'll get the rim later.'

They jumped to push Janus to the road, but as they did so, Janus once more held up his hand for silence. 'Listen,' he said. For a moment there was no sound; then there came a faint clanging and jingling. But it came from the opposite direction of the screams. 'Oh, it's only the tin man's wagon,' Jella said at last.

They shoved Janus into the road. 'Hold it,' he said. 'Wait for the wagon. It will get us to the women a lot quicker than we can get there on foot.'

Down the canal road the horse and wagon came, around a bend and over the bridge in full gallop. The pots and pans danced and jangled, clattered and banged.

'Hey, look,' Pier said. 'Isn't that Auka on the seat? He's standing up. He looks as if he's yelling at us.'

Auka had been sitting between the tin man and his wife on the high seat of the old wagon. The children had settled down in the deep wagon box among the pots and pans. The tin man had insisted on taking them for a long ride around Shora—the direct route down the dike road from Nes to Shora had been too short for him. Everybody deserved an outing this Saturday, he had insisted. They'd ended up on the canal road on the opposite side of Shora.

As they rounded the bend in the road and came over the canal bridge, Auka caught sight of the little group at the canal. 'Look!' Auka yelled out. 'Something's wrong! Somebody must have drowned. Even Janus is there in the wheel chair.' He jumped up on the seat. 'Can this horse run?' he asked anxiously.

'He can run that far,' the tin man said. He slapped the lines hard across the horse's bony back. The old horse lunged ahead. With an insane jangling of tin, the wagon lurched and rattled toward the waiting group at the roadside.

CHAPTER X

Wagon in the Sea

'Is SOMETHING wrong?' Auka shouted out above the rattling, clanging din as the wagon neared the group around the wheel chair at the side of the road. The wagon stopped. The tin stopped banging.

'Yes, something's wrong but not here,' Janus said. 'We heard women screaming on the dike somewhere the other side of the village. We were just going there.'

'Well, jump on,' the tin man said, 'and we'll get you there as fast as the old horse will go. Hey, that's right, you in the wheel chair can't do much jumping. Maybe we can all hoist you up, and . . .'

'Don't sit there, man, with foolish plans in your mouth,' Janus interrupted him. 'Get going to that dike! Just give me a chance to grab the back end of the wagon; I'll come on behind some way.'

It was a crazy procession that stormed into Shora and along the road to the dike. The old horse tried to make speed as best he could, but the added weight of his new passengers slowed him down. But the wagon looked fast, and the tin made it sound faster. The wagon hobbling and bouncing over the big cobble-stones was one hideous clangour of tin. The pots and pans swung wildly on their wires. Janus in the wheel chair rolled on behind.

Janus had taken a stout grip with both hands on the back of the wagon. The rope around his chest kept him from bouncing out of his chair. He was riding almost under the wagon; only his head and shoulders poked up from behind. The teacher and Jella ran beside the wheel chair, straining and panting to keep the bouncing chair upright. 'So long as the wheels don't come off,' the teacher said.

Janus was in fine fettle; he wasn't worrying about the wheels. From behind the wagon he was trying to urge the horse on still faster. 'Hola, hola, hola,' he kept bellowing to the old horse.

'Hi, tell him back there not to shout "hola"!' the tin man yelled. 'It sounds too much like "whoa" to the horse.'

'Nobody tells Janus anything,' Auka told the tin man.

In spite of the 'hola's ', the horse seemed to respond to the excitement in Janus's voice. His bony rump went still higher; his big feet pounded heavily over the cobblestones. He went ahead—at full speed for him—and he carried his load out of the village.

The women on the dike stood staring in mute un-belief at the loaded tinware wagon as it came storming and banging toward them. Somewhere behind the wagon the voice of the unseen Janus bellowed out above the din. All the women were back on the dike. A farmer was coming with horses and wagon to rescue Lina and Douwa. The women had not waited for him to hitch his horses to a wagon before they'd run back to the dike.

Lina's mother was the first to come to her senses. She dashed down to open the gate that led to the dike path. The dike path was a narrow wagon lane that had been dug on a long gradual slant into the side of the dike. On this path a wagon could mount alongside the steep dike to the top. The Wagon ran through the gate and up the long slant of the dike path. The climb slowed the old horse immediately. In a totally flat country he wasn't used to pulling uphill. He coughed and quivered, he strained with all his bony strength, but the wagon wheels barely turned.

Janus yelled, 'Hola, hola, hola.' It did no good. The horse had given his all; he was too old and sensible to attempt the impossible. He let Janus yell, and the wagon wheels ground practically to a standstill.

It was too much for Janus. 'Everybody off but the driver and the little kids,' he ordered. 'And everybody push. Old Bonerack 's had all he can take, and he's got to have some help. He did all right.' Janus was almost trying to push the wagon ahead from his wheel chair. All the boys jumped down from the wagon. Even the tin man vaulted from the high seat, and his wife took the reins.

Up on top of the dike Jana stood struck speechless, too surprised to do anything but stare. But as the wagon neared the crest of the dike, she found her voice. 'Was that my Janus? Did I hear Janus's voice?'

Then the wagon came over the dike and rolled to a stop before the women. Janus came from behind it in the wheel chair, proudly pushing himself toward his astounded wife. He was triumphant. 'Sure, it's Janus! Who did you think it was—Santa Claus?'

'No, but it's as good as Santa Claus,' the woman said softly.

Janus looked away from her and spun his wheel chair around to look at the sea. He took in the situation of old Douwa and Lina stranded, knee-deep in water now, on top of the upturned boat. Once again he stared far out to sea. He sat there almost quivering. He snuffed in the tangy sea air, opening his mouth wide and breathing it deep. Here he was on the dike with the sea below thundering in full tide. Here he was in the midst of things again.

He shook his head to shake off the mood and then took command. 'Off with all the kids and tin here on top of the dike,' he said. 'We can't have the tin man's wares get rusty from salt water, but we've got to use the wagon to get the old man and the girl. Everybody get busy. But use your heads. If I still know my sea and my tides, we've got half an hour before those two on the boat go under. So pile the stuff neatly, and don't knock dents into it or scatter it all over the place.'

All the women and the boys rushed to unload the wagon. But one of the women remembered the farmer. She rushed away to tell him he and his wagon would not be needed now.

'Hey, tin man!' Janus yelled. 'Will your horse go into the sea, or would it scare him spitless?'

'Not him,' the tin man said promptly. 'He's used to the sea. If I'm near the sea, I take him into the salt water almost every day to tighten and heal his old flat feet from the road sores. He loves it.'

'Ah, good,' Janus said. He studied the big feet of the horse. 'Yes, I can see. He's a willing old skate. Does his best. His splay feet should come in handy, at least he shouldn't sink into the silt when he's got to tug the wagon into the sea—not on those snowshoe feet of his.'

Behind Janus, the women and boys had the wagon empty. The neat piles of tin pots and saucepans stood in an orderly row on the top of the dike. Beyond the piles stood a soldierlike row of coffee pots which wouldn't stack. Beyond the coffee pots the pieces of tin, which the tin man used to patch old pots and pans, were piled beside his box of tools.

Janus ran his eyes over everything and saw that all was in order. 'Fine,' he said. 'Now into the sea. Just you,' he told the tin man. 'No load. It's better for the horse if the wagon floats, and you two are used to each other.'

The wagon started slowly down the dike toward the sea, with the old horse hanging his weight against the pushing weight behind him. Now they noticed that on top of the upturned boat Lina had begun frantically waving her hand at them. Douwa stood beside her, holding her. He seemed to be instructing Lina.

'Quiet, everybody,' Janus cried. 'They're trying to tell us something.' The tin man stopped the wagon halfway down the dike. Everybody leaned forward to hear the long-screamed-out words that came from the boat over the thundering tide. Lina stopped shouting and turned to the old man as if for further instructions. She began shouting out each word even more slowly this time and shriller and higher.

Janus waved both his hands high above his head. 'It's all right, little girl,' he bellowed over the waves. 'I got it, Janus will fix it.'

'Listen,' came the drawn-out, shrill words. 'Listen, Janus. It's not just Douwa and me—there's a wagon wheel. And it's got to be pulled through a hole in the bottom of this boat. The wagon's got to come right over the boat and over the hole. *So the wheels have to come off the wagon.*'

Janus waved his hand cheerily. 'It's all right, little girl,' he called back so hard that the cords in his neck stood out. 'Don't you worry. Janus will pull that wheel out for you.'

Lina and the old man waved to show they'd understood.

For a moment there was excited chatter on the dike. 'Lina's got a wheel,' the amazed boys told each other. 'Lina 's found a wheel. Found a wheel in a boat! She went and looked in a boat for a wheel.'

'It's crazy,' Jella summed it up for all of them.

But Janus turned on them. 'What are you? Magpies? Cut out the chatter. Tin man,' he shouted to the wagon on the side of the dike, 'have you got a wagon jack?'

'Of course,' the tin man said. 'With a wagon like mine and the wheels I've got, you need a jack almost as much as you need a horse. But I don't think we'll need a jack. The wheels come off easy—they've been on and off so often. If I just drive into the tide, the horse and the water will hold the wagon up enough so we can pull the hind wheels off. It'll be quicker.'

'Good,' Janus said. 'If it's quicker that's what we'll do; we've no time to waste. As the tide gets higher and the tide current begins to hit their legs, those two will find it harder and harder to keep their footing on that slimy boat. It could sweep them off.'

Janus wasn't satisfied until everybody but the women was busy with the wheels. The teacher was ordered to wade waist-deep into the sea to help the tin man with the front wheels. They were the only two tall enough to risk the depth of the tide water that far from the dike. The boys worked on the back wheels. With everybody busy, Janus studied the sea again and the half-submerged figures of the old man and the girl standing in the rushing water. 'Well,' he said to the women, 'look at that. There stands that little bun of a girl, and she isn't a bit panicky, up there to her little belly in the cold water. Who did all the screaming a while back, before we came?'

'That bun of a girl is my daughter,' Lina's mother said quietly. 'And we did all the screaming. She isn't panicky because of old Douwa, and we aren't panicky now either, you may have noticed. We got desperate because we didn't know what to do. But now you're here, there's a wagon, and you seem to know exactly what to do. And now I'm not worried.'

Janus went red with pleasure. 'Those are kind words, Lena,' he said thickly. 'You don't know how kind.' He looked at his wife. Then he saw that all the wheels had been pulled off the wagon. The boys were rolling them up the dike. The back of the wagon rested against the slant of the dike. The horse stood flank-deep in the sea.

'Down with the tail gate,' Janus told the teacher. He propelled himself down the slant of the dike and rode over the open tail gate into the wagon. 'Come on,' he called. 'Everybody on but the women and tots. We're going to need weight now to hold the wagon in place above that boat if we're to get that wheel out. Hurry!'

His wife stepped toward the wagon. 'Janus, do you think——?' She bit her tongue to cut off the words. Her whole body went rigid as she forced herself to say no more. The boys piled into the wagon. The teacher pulled the tail gate up and fastened it in place. The tin man was already on the high seat. He clucked to the horse. The horse started tugging, but the wheelless rear axle dug into the foot of the dike. All the women hurried forward and half lifting, half pushing, they freed the back end of the wagon. The horse tugged it into the sea. Now the wagon box floated free. It swung and swayed behind the horse as he breasted the tide.

At the foot of the dike Jana stood wordlessly looking at the swaying, swinging wagon. Her nervous fingers kept digging into her apron pocket as she fought to keep from saying one anxious word. Janus was so excited, so happy. There he sat like a king among the excited, chattering boys. After a moment Jana looked down at what she was doing. Her fingers in her pocket were rooting among the smooth stones that she had picked up along her bread route that day. They were extra smooth and round, extra special ones for Janus to throw at birds and boys. She pulled them out and looked at them. One by one she dropped them at her feet. Then she looked at the floating wagon. 'Bring them all back safely, Janus—wheel and all,' she suddenly called out.

'I will, I will, Jana,' Janus answered her. 'You just leave it to Janus.'

Jana smiled nervously and kicked at the little pile of stones at her feet. Lina's mother thoughtfully watched the wagon on the sea. Jana looked up at her. 'He'll bring your Lina back,' Jana assured her. She was quietly proud.

In the sea the old horse suddenly lost his footing. The tide had swept his feet from under him. He pawed and snorted and coughed. Then he was swimming. He coughed once more, threw his head back from the rolling waves, and swam on. He didn't panic in the least. Janus looked at the old horse admiringly. 'You know what, tin man? When this is all over, Shora owes your horse a big bushel of oats. Doesn't he, lads?'

'Two bushels,' they shouted.

'Well, see to it as soon as possible,' Janus said. 'You'll see that they do it, Teacher?'

'Yes, Janus.'

They came nearer the submerged boat. The rounded bottom was completely under the tide water. Douwa and Lina were standing waist-deep and chest-deep in the water over the boat. They were clutching each other to keep their footing against the steady tug of the tide. Fortunately the stern of the boat broke the force of the tide and sent the full strength of its current sweeping along both sides of the boat. But the slimy boat provided an insecure foothold. The two on the boat never moved their eyes from the coming wagon.

'Lina, did you really find a wagon wheel?' Auka shouted from the wagon.

Lina forgot her plight in her pride. 'Yes,' she answered back. 'A really big one, and it's really good.

135

The salt water kept it perfect. But it's so waterlogged. Grandpa Douwa and I couldn't budge it.'

The wagon had now drawn so close they could hear the old man say to Lina, 'And what did I tell you about that "grandpa" stuff?'

Lina giggled.

The boys were asking questions. Janus sternly silenced them. 'Time for all that when you're back on the dike. Now shut your magpie mouths. Better take the horse and wagon beyond the boat,' he told the tin man, 'then we can let the wagon box float back over the boat. If all of us are enough of a load, maybe we can ground the axles against the boat bottom long enough to pull up the wheel.'

The tin man nodded and tugged at the reins to execute the tricky manœuvre in the tide current. Janus turned his attention to Douwa. 'As the wagon backs toward you and Lina, grab and climb on. We'll help pull you in. But watch that you don't step into that hole in the boat. Look, Douwa, do you know exactly where that hole is, so that we can find its edge and not get the wagon box too far over it? It's got to be a straight pull to get that wheel out.'

'Thought of that, Janus, and marked it with a buoy.' Douwa cheerfully pointed to his stick floating out before him. 'Tied the rope that's tied to the wheel to my cane.'

Janus laughed. 'Good for you.' he said approvingly.

Now everything went tense—everybody was silent. The wagon had swung ahead of the boat, but the tin man was having difficulty in getting the horse to stop his hard swimming and to allow the current to sweep the wagon backward over the boat to Douwa and Lina. The whole instinct of the animal was to swim with all his might against the tide. He snorted and fought; he did not want to drift helplessly backward on the current. The tin man spoke soothing words, all kinds of soft understanding cluckings. They knew each other from all the years. The old horse began to listen and to relax. The wagon started drifting backward toward Douwa and Lina. The old man and Lina leaned forward, reached out, now they both grabbed the wagon box. Eager hands reached out of the wagon and pulled them in. Up they came together.

In the back of the wagon, tight against the tail gate, Janus sat, intent on the floating stick. Now the wagon neared it. 'Everybody to the back end,' Janus said. 'We've got to weigh it down and try to make the axle dig into the keel of the boat to stop the wagon.'

Everybody crowded around Janus. Their weight was enough. Suddenly the wagon stopped and settled down on the keel of the boat. The horse was still swimming. 'Keep him swimming just enough that he holds the wagon straight,' Janus said. 'It mustn't swing around in the current.'

'That's exactly what we're doing,' the tin man shouted. 'But be quick back there; the horse is tiring.'

'Get down, you, and grab that stick,' Janus told Jella. 'No, don't think about it. Flat on your belly in the water in the wagon box and grab.'

Jella came spluttering to his knees with the stick in his hand. Janus grabbed it from him. 'Now everybody hang on to my chair and up with that wheel.' Janus was pulling in the rope as he talked. He took a new grip as the rope tightened with the weight of the wheel. The chair began creaking. Janus's great arms bulged. The creak of the chair was the only sound above the rushing of the tide. The wheel began coming up. Suddenly it caught against the edge of the hole.

Janus muttered, got red-faced and fierce, and then, with a mighty heave and a tug, he freed the wheel. Up rose the rim of the wheel out of the water.

But Janus's violent struggles had loosened the axle from its dug-in hold on the rotted keel of the old boat.

Suddenly the wagon pushed backward out over the hole, and the wheel started to go under the wagon.

'Teacher, Douwa, grab the rope,' Janus yelled. 'Just hold! Hold the wheel from sinking back. Tin man, make that horse pull with all he's got. Kids, all you kids, tip my chair down to the water. Come on, tip it! I won't fall out; I'm tied in. Tip it, I say.'

They all obeyed. Janus, wheel chair, and all tipped down toward the water. He strained against the ropes around his chest. He reached as far as he could down under the wagon and the water. 'Just so I get one finger on that wheel,' he said. And then he had it, had it with both hands. His arms strained and swelled. 'Now tip me back,' he ordered. The boys pulled, the teacher flung his arms around Janus's chest, and Douwa, even Lina, grabbed Janus and the back of the chair. Up came the chair and, clutched in Janus's big hands, up came the wheel. After his chair stood straight again, he swung the wheel up over his head, held it there triumphantly, and stared up at it. 'Hey,' he grunted between his teeth, 'a man can do something now and then without a lot of legs.' Then he let the wheel down, and they took it from him and lowered it to the bottom of the wagon.

'It's done,' he yelled at the tin man. 'It's done. Now give old Bonerack his head. Now he can go with the current, and the wagon will push him to shore. Poor old fellow . . .' The horse swung. The wagon swung. Horse and wagon swung around and swept toward the dike at the speed of the onrushing tide. The old horse merely had to move his legs to keep himself upright.

From the dike came the excited cries of the women. They were crowded together at the edge of the water. They waved their arms and cheered. The dike loomed closer and closer before the wagon in the sea. The tide swept them on toward the solid dike which rose like the wall of a great fort above the thundering sea.

138

The Storm and the Storks

THE storm came that Saturday night. Deep in the dark, wind-swept night, the storm roared up against the dike and over the roofs of Shora. The wind thundered up out of the North Sea, howled down the narrow street of Shora, shrieked under the heavy roof tiles, and made roaring sounds down the wide chimneys—the roar of a giant. The children of Shora slept.

Lina slept alone in the attic, directly under the roof tiles. A sweep of wind slashing under the tiles lifted some of the heavy tiles and tossed them up like paper. They crashed back down on the roof, smashed, and went slithering down the steep roof to shatter into a thousand pieces on the cobblestone street. The attic beams groaned. A moaning, wolfish howl of wind ran down the chimney and through the trembling house. Lina woke suddenly. For long moments she lay absolutely still, trying to interpret the giant sounds that rushed and rolled through the attic. She did not understand in that first foggy lift out of deep sleep. She couldn't make her mind work.

139

Suddenly she quivered. There were tripping, running noises over the attic floor. Something alive was in the attic with her and was running over the floor. Her skin crawled. She did not even dare to twist her head toward the sound, afraid that her slightest movement would give her presence away. She stared straight up, eyes big with horror. At last her slow senses seemed to come back despite her frozen scare and told her the running, tripping noise was rain—wind-swept raindrops hurtling through the spaces where the roof tiles had been ripped off by the wind.

She heard voices outside in the storm. The wind caught them up, swept and swirled the bodiless voices up over the roofs. They penetrated to the attic, but they were senseless, meaningless. The wind thundered in the chimney again, rattled the roof tiles, and drowned out the eerie night voices.

Gradually Lina understood that the storm old Douwa had predicted had come. Somewhere out there in the deep of night were voices screaming on the dike. People yelled at each other against the thunder of the waves and wind. The wind made voices sound hopeless and helpless—like the cries of a wounded animal.

Lina couldn't stay in bed. The attic was cold, draughty, and rain-swept; it chilled Lina the moment she let herself down the side of the high box bed. But she let herself drop and ran on bare feet to the attic window. Lina looked up. She saw patches of dim, confused storm light where the roof tiles were gone. The rain fell through the openings.

Lina heard no voices now. But on the dike she saw moving, flickering lights. Lanterns! People with lanterns were on the dike. Now the wind caught a woman's sharp high voice and swept it from the dike to the attic. The lanterns tossed and swung in the unseen hands that held them.

The next moment there came such a complete lull in the wind, it was as if it had been cut off, as if a great door had closed on it. In the lull Lina heard men's voices. Men were shouting on the dike! Then she realized—the fishing fleet was in! The fleet had got home before the full storm, and now they were unloading and making the boats safe. The women of Shora must be helping their men. But all Lina could see was the feeble light of the moving lanterns.

Right below her window in the black street, somebody called out so suddenly and unexpectedly, Lina jerked back from the window. Then she realized the voice was her father's. Her father was down there shouting to someone, 'Yes, everybody got in safe but not a moment too soon.'

He must have been shouting to old Douwa, for now came her mother's sharper voice urging Douwa to go back in his house—not to go out to the dike. 'The wind knocks you down. I came over the dike on hands and knees, and if I hadn't been dragging a heavy basket with fish—well, it was all that held me on the dike. Don't risk your old bones, Douwa.'

For a second the words of her mother stood there clear and precise in the darkness, then the wind crashed down and the attic roared and shook. Then the murmur of voices in the house below came faintly up to Lina in the attic. Her mother and father had come into the house. Lina turned to rush down the ladder to greet her father. But she was chilled and wet —even her hair. She'd crawl into bed. She'd get warm and dry first, then she'd run down. The murmur went on down below.

Lina hurried back to bed, skirting the wet spots on the attic floor. She was so cold she had difficulty reaching up to catch the top board to draw herself up into the high box bed. Teeth chattering, she slid into bed. After the chill and the damp, the bed was so warm and enveloping, she lay for a while almost enjoying the little after-shivers that unexpectedly came up and raced all through her. She felt her damp hair; she'd better crawl right under the clothes if her hair was going to dry.

When Lina woke, the covers were still over her head. Her first gesture was to feel her hair—it was dry. But when she tossed the clothes back, it was light in the attic. It was daylight, the confused, troubled light of a dark stormy day. She had slept all night through the storm. She hadn't gone down to her father; she'd fallen asleep. The rain still fell. The wind still roared above the house; it came in jerky moaning howls down the big chimney. It was still storming, but it somehow sounded different in the daylight, not so bone-chilling and terrifying. Maybe, Lina thought hopefully, it was even dying down. Maybe it would blow over. If it did, then tomorrow, Monday, they could put the wheel on the school.

Lina jumped from the high bed to rush down to her father. She yelped when her bare feet hit the cold, wet floor. She stood a moment on one foot trying to warm the sole of her other foot against her leg. As she stood balancing, she could see from the high attic window the dirty grey spume sliding over the top of the dike. Flecks of it were flying through the air. Behind the dike the great waves thundered high, and a black sky hung where the islands were supposed to be. There were no islands. It was a real storm. It was Sunday. With a shiver, Lina grabbed all her clothes from the chair and in her nightgown rushed down the attic ladder.

Lina did not get to see her father before church-time. She had a glimpse of his face in the high box bed set in the wall of the living room—that part of his face between his chin and nose that was not covered by the blankets and his sleeping cap with the long, dangling tassel. He had drawn his sleeping cap far over his eyes to shut out the light. The tassel hung over his mouth. It quivered and fluttered there as he breathed in deep, exhausted sleep. Lina tiptoed out of the living room toward the sounds of frying in the kitchen.

The wind coming down the chimney roared and bellowed in the stove. Lina's mother at the stove did not hear her come in. 'I don't suppose Dad is going to church?' Lina said loudly. 'He looks as if he could sleep a week.'

Her mother turned. 'Oh, he'll be there. You can believe he'll be there out of sheer gratitude for beating that storm to shore. They had a night of it out there in the sea. I'm letting him sleep every minute . . .'

The wind roared down the chimney and blotted out her words. Oddly above the wind's roar the cry of a single seagull came down the chimney. The gull must have been flying high over the house.

'Even the gulls are being driven inland, and that means a real storm,' Lina's mother said, listening to it.

Now there were cries of other gulls, eerie and high and wind-swept. 'Listen to them,' Lina said. 'They sound scared. But, Mum, if even the gulls can't hold out against the storm, what's going to happen to the poor storks? They're so big, the wind would really hit them hard.'

'I suppose they'll settle down here and there and wait out the storm. They're clever.'

'But over the sea? When they come over the sea?' Lina asked.

Lina's mother shrugged and turned her attention to the fish she was frying on the stove. 'You and I'll just have breakfast. I'll let him sleep to the last minute and send him off to church with a cup of tea. He'll be too tired to eat anyway. And I'm keeping your little sister at home. Linda 's too small to go through that.'

Her mother wasn't paying any attention to her, Lina thought. When breakfast was set before her, she gulped the food without noticing what she was eating.

'What's your hurry, and where's your mind?' her mother said impatiently, sitting down at the table across from her.

'Mum, I'm worried about the storks. I want to go to church early. Is it all right if I don't wait for you? Maybe some of the boys will be there, and we've got to work out about the wheel. But what if the storks are scattered by the storm?'

'Lina, I've got to confess that just now I can't be worried about a stork. I'm too busy being grateful that your father and all the others got back safely! I'm saying little prayers. But those animals have sense and instincts; no doubt they feel a storm coming long before we people know it. They'll do what needs to be done before the storm overtakes them. Oh, I don't know. But you just hurry on to church and talk it out of your system.'

Lina flew to get dressed in her Sunday best. But her mother insisted she wear her storm jacket over her Sunday dress and also wear her stocking cap! 'There's rain squalls whipping up and down the whole street. You'd be soaked through in a minute, and all you can keep on is a stocking cap.'

Lina grumbled but did not argue; she was too eager to get to church. When she stepped out of the door the force of the wind awed her. It jerked the door out of her hand and slammed it shut with such violence that the bang of the door seemed to shake the whole house. She had to bend into the wind. Stooped like a little old woman, she forced her way into the wind that came in wild screams around corners and howled along the walls of the houses down the narrow street. She was glad now of the jacket and stocking cap as the wind ripped at her—anything else the wind would have torn off her.

As Lina staggered toward the church porch, a face was cautiously poked through the open entrance. It was Eelka. Lina pulled herself up the two steps. All the boys were already there, huddled for a little shelter in the partly enclosed porch. Lina stood a moment gasping for breath. The boys gathered around her.

'We've been waiting,' Eelka said soberly. 'Have you thought of what this is going to do to the storks? They're all on their way out of Africa by now, and if this storm caught them, they'll be blown all over Europe.'

'If they don't go down in the sea,' Jella added.

'I know,' Lina said hopelessly. 'Even the seagulls can't fight it. It's awful.'

'But what can you do?' Pier said. 'Just hope it doesn't storm too much tomorrow. Boy, with the fleet in, all our dads could help us get the wheel up. If we could get *them* to help tomorrow, then we'd be ready for any stork that manages to come along after the storm.'

'Yes, Pier,' Auka said eagerly. 'That's an idea! Get all our dads to help—that wheel weighs a ton. I don't think even the five of us could get it up ladders and slide it on the roof. I know. I helped put up a wheel in Nes, and that was a worn-out, dried-out, old thing . . .'

'That's what we'll do,' Lina said excitedly. 'We'll all ask our dads. They'll help when they hear about our stork plans for Shora! When it's storming, they've nothing else to do anyway. They'll be glad enough for something to do.'

'If it doesn't storm so hard that nobody can get up on a roof,' Jella said forebodingly. 'You know how it goes with our dads. The storm might blow itself out during the night. Then if it's calm, away they go to sea again. We've got to catch them tomorrow even if it's still stormy.'

'Teacher would let us,' Dirk said. 'He said last night there'd be no school on Monday if we could get the wheel up. Of course, he didn't reckon on a storm.'

'He even let us put the wheel in school,' Pier told Lina. 'So that it would dry out a little, and because Auka was so worried somebody might steal it.'

'When?' Lina demanded, resenting having been left out of things. After all, it was she who had found the wheel!

'Oh, we did all that after your mother took you in the house, because you'd been in the cold water so long on that boat,' Pier told Lina. 'After your mother took you home, we still had to put the wheels back on and reload the wagon—only everybody bought something from the tin man as sort of thanks for helping so. Dirk and me even sneaked some oats for the horse out of that barn where we got the hay—sort of for thanks, too.'

'Sneaked,' Lina said resentfully. 'Stole!'

'Well, he had it coming,' Pier said smartly. 'And it was only a couple of stocking capfuls.'

Lina's thoughts were already back with the wheel in the school. 'Do you suppose we should ask the teacher if we can build a fire in the stove in school and put the wheel up close to it to dry? It's been under water over eighty years, Douwa told me, except when the tide was out. That's what makes it so heavy. Douwa told me a lot of things when we were on the boat together.'

'Douwa told *me* not to dry it too fast, or it would shrink so much it might fall apart—just like Eelka's wheel,' Jella said. 'Douwa and I talked a lot about the wheel last night.' Jella wasn't going to be outdone by Lina.

146

Lina had the words in her mouth for further things she'd learned from old Douwa, but they had to move away from the church door. The janitress arrived. It was Douwa's granddaughter, Janka. They had been so busy planning and plotting and arguing they had not seen her come. Janka unlocked the door. They trooped into the damp, empty church behind her and started to sit down in the back pew that was reserved for children.

'I don't know,' Janka said, seeing them sitting down, 'but it looks to me as if you will be the whole congregation. Only a seagull and a kid can breast a storm like this. I don't see how I got here.'

'My father's coming if my mother can wake him up,' Lina said to her.

'All our dads are,' Jella said. 'My dad said that when you come out of a sea like that and step on a solid dike, you want to go to church right then and there. They'll be here.'

'Yes, I suppose so,' Janka said. 'Along with all their thankful wives. I had to argue myself warm to keep my grandfather Douwa from coming.' She moved off, but before disappearing through a door at the front of the church, she called back, 'Behave yourselves now. This is a church.'

It was a temptation. That is, it would have been a temptation any other time when left to themselves to gallop around and play hide-and-seek in an empty church with not a single stern adult to hinder them. But they were too worried about the storks in the storm and too full of their plans for the wheel. Suddenly they couldn't sit still any longer with their worries in the silent, cold church. Auka at the aisle end of the pew got up and moved back to the porch; immediately everybody followed him. In the porch they kept sticking their heads around the projecting piers to look down the street.

147

At last people were coming—the women first. They came on, stooped into the wind, bent almost double. All the women carried wooden footstoves with small pots of glowing coals inside to warm their feet in the fireless church. The wind caught the glowing coals inside the stoves, sending showers of flying sparks down the street. One woman hastily set her footstove down and with her Psalter beat out a spark that had caught in her woollen shawl. The wind ripped at the full skirts of the women.

Farther down the street came the fishermen. They had been to the dike in the wind and storm to look to the safety of their boats and to study sky and sea before cooping themselves up in church.

Jella pulled the church door open for the women with their sparking stoves. The women came in, breathless from the push against the wind. They stumbled gratefully into the church, their eyes thanking Jella.

Now the men approached. The boys and Lina studied the sombre faces of the men. 'Will the storm last long?' Auka asked.

'Days,' a man said. The others nodded. 'A week, maybe.' They hurried into the church, in no mood for small talk.

Now there was nothing left to wait for. The congregation was inside. Nothing came down the wind-swept street but a gull's piercing, lonely cry. Dirk peered out a last time before going into church. 'Teacher isn't coming, I reckon. I wanted to ask him about Monday morning . . . Hey!' he whispered excitedly. 'Who do you think is coming to church? Janus! Why, he hasn't been inside a church—— But Jana has all she can do to push his wheel chair ahead in that wind. Come on, let's help her.' Lina and the boys dashed into the street. 'We'll help you,' they shouted to Jana.

But Jana wouldn't let them help. 'Not this time,'

148

she said in a low breathless voice. 'No, this isn't the time. I've got to push him this first time.'

The boys did help to lift the wheel chair up the two steps to the porch.

'Not too far down the aisle now,' Janus warned Jana. 'Not up to the pulpit, I'm not going to preach the sermon. Let's stay at the back a little. I don't want them all to get heart failure—Janus in church!'

'Put the chair next to the children's pew,' Lina begged. 'That's at the back.'

'So long as it's at the back,' Janus said.

Jana had to sit on the women's side of the church, but the children's pew was the last one on the men's side. The boys took over from Jana. They wheeled Janus smartly to the end of their pew, but then each one tried to manœuvre so as to get to be the one to sit next to Janus. Big Jella was the winner. Lina got the seat farthest away, tight against the damp, chilly wall. 'Ask Janus,' she whispered. 'Ask him if he thinks the storm will last and if there'll be any more storks coming if the storm lasts long.'

They whispered the question from mouth to mouth along the pew. Jella put the problem to Janus.

Janus turned and looked at Jella in disgust. 'What nonsense!' he said aloud then suddenly remembered he was in church. 'Nonsense,' he whispered hoarsely. All the children leaned forward to hear every word. 'What are you kids worrying about?' Janus said disgustedly. 'Those few storks you saw so far are just the advance guard—the old-timers who are getting slow and need an early start. The young stuff is still coming. The real trek has still got to come. They'll come by hundreds.'

'Are you sure, Janus?' Lina whispered from the end of the pew. It sounded too good to be true.

'Sure?' Janus's whisper exploded. 'Why do you suppose I've been watching birds for all these years? I

149

would practically know all the storks that fly over by name—if they didn't have such outlandish African names.'

The whole bench exploded with giggles that couldn't be suppressed. Indignant heads turned, then stayed turned in amazement at Janus in church. Janus became aware of the people staring at him. His face went red. He hastily snatched off his cap and held it before his face to pray into as he had seen the other men doing. Behind his cap Janus did not see the sensation he was causing. People nudged each other and jerked their heads toward the back of the church. 'Janus is in church!' One by one they looked around a second time as if to make sure they'd seen right the first time. There were more whispers.

Janus peeked from behind his cap and saw the heads turning toward him and the children's bench. Without warning he took the astonished Jella by the shoulder and shook him hard. 'Hush, you kids,' he said fiercely. 'Can't you behave in church? Hush, I say . . . but there'll be a lot more storks coming after the storm. Hush!'

His wife, sitting three benches ahead, turned around to give Janus a warning look, but he was too busy scolding the children and whispering his information. 'Janus! Hush yourself now!' Jana warned in a hissing whisper. 'The dominie is mounting the pulpit.'

Janus let go of Jella's shoulder and sat meekly staring up at the old dominie in the high pulpit. Jella rubbed his sore shoulder, and then he, too, sat as quietly as the other children—reassured now and calmed by Janus's promise of more storks to come.

CHAPTER XII

The Wheel
on the School

ON MONDAY morning the storm hadn't stopped. It raged in fury against the dike. The sea was up-ended; the spume and roiled spindrift still flew high above the dike, landing in grey dirty flecks in the streets and on the roofs. If anything, the storm was more jerky and fitful. Odd sudden lulls seemed to fall momentarily between the high shrieks and moans of the wind, although behind the dike the sea thundered on. Enormous breakers hurled themselves up and washed in a last, thin, hissing line almost to the crest of the dike. Now and then the spent water of an unusually large wave managed to spill over the dike.

In the houses the fishermen sat loafing in the corners of their kitchens, behind the stoves if possible, to be out of the way of their busy wives and of their

151

children getting ready for school. They were given no peace. In all Shora the fishermen fathers were pestered by their children. The wheel had to go up on the school, storm or no storm.

'Just suppose some storks came through tomorrow,' Lina argued with her father in the kitchen.

'Yes, just suppose and suppose,' her father barked back. 'Just suppose you let me be nice and quiet in my little corner. It feels good to be dry and warm and to do nothing for a change.'

'Yes, but just suppose the storm ends, then you'll be going out to sea again, and we won't have a wheel up on the roof of the school. There's nobody else but Janus and old Douwa, and they can't get on roofs.'

'They're lucky!' her father said impatiently. 'It'll be a long storm, I've told you. There's plenty of time. That storm isn't just going to shut off like a tap. Can't I wait at least for a quieter day?' He disappeared behind his week-old newspaper, which, since he had been at sea for weeks, was news to him—news and a refuge to hide behind.

He was given no chance to read it. Lina's little sister, Linda, at that moment insisted on climbing into his lap, and on the other side of the newspaper Lina still argued with him. 'Teacher said on Saturday that if the wheel could go up today, there'd be no school. So we can all help you,' she said to the newspaper. 'With all of us helping, it shouldn't take long.'

'What does that teacher know about wind and storms? Let him get on that roof in a storm then! And it's off to school with you right now. There'll come a quieter day before we can take off for sea again, and then we'll see. But off with you, so I can have a quiet day today.'

It was final. Lina indignantly shoved her feet into her wooden shoes. She knew better than to argue further. She had gone as far as she dared. She buttoned

152

her jacket tightly up around her throat and stamped out of the house.

'Listen, Jella, how often do I have to tell you? I'm not stirring from this house today, and that's final. A man ought to have a few days of rest after weeks out at sea without having to sit on top of a school. Now be off! Get into that school and learn something instead of sitting on top of it.'

'But the teacher said there'd be no school today if we put the wheel up.'

'Well, you can't get the wheel up in this storm, so there is school, and I say so. Or do I have to take you there by the scruff of your neck and the seat of your pants?'

Jella shoved his feet disgustedly into his wooden shoes and slammed the door hard behind him.

'Listen, Pier and Dirk—that's the trouble with twins, a man gets a double dose of everything—one more yammer or argument out of the two of you, and I'll knock your two heads together so hard you'll be lucky if you have one head left between you. Even so, that ought to be enough—you don't use your two heads. The answer is: No, No, NO! NO wheel on NO school in NO storm!'

'But we'd help all you men. The teacher said no school if . . .'

'And I say there is school, and you two will be in it if only so that I don't have to hear another word about storks. On your way!'

Pier and Dirk looked at each other. They glumly shoved their feet into their shoes and moved to the door, muttering dire things to each other. Behind his week-old newspaper their father sat grinning at their fuming threats. 'Learn your lesson well today,' he teased them. 'I hear it's going to be about storks.'

153

'It might be about lazy, stubborn fishermen,' Pier said stormily. Afraid he'd said too much, he scooted to the door with Dirk close behind him. Their father rustled the newspaper. Dirk pushed Pier through the door and almost stumbled over him to get out as fast as he could. The door fell shut.

'Listen, Auka, don't you ever let me alone? If I hear another word about another stork, I'll . . . I'll take your neck and stretch it until you look like a stork. Then *you* can go and sit up on a wheel on top of a roof. Storks got more sense than to do that in a storm. How do you expect me to lug a wheel up that roof in a storm? I haven't got wings! And if I should slide down a slippery roof in this high wind and land on my head, who's going to earn the money so that you can go to school and fool around with storks? You get to that school!'

'But there is no school if we put the wheel up.'

'Well, nobody is going to put that wheel up today, so there is school. Goodbye, Auka.'

There was nothing left for Auka to do but to put his shoes on and move off silently. His father watched him. 'If you stick that lower lip out much farther in your pout, you can put that wagon wheel on there instead of on the roof,' he teased.

Auka said a few wicked things to himself and looked stonily at his father as he closed the door very slowly to let in as much wind and draught as possible.

Eelka's father, sitting cosily beside the stove in the kitchen, peered around his newspaper to watch Eelka slowly putting on his shoes, buttoning his jacket, and pulling up the collar. 'Where do you think you're going, son?'

'To school,' Eelka said. 'It's Monday, you know, but it's much too stormy to put that wheel up on the roof of the school today. So I suppose it'll be school.' He sighed. 'I never did have much luck.'

Eelka hunched himself to meet the wind that was driving down the street. Ahead of him were all the other school children, bent over, boring into the wind. Unwilling and angry and defeated, each one walked alone on the hard way to school. No one hurried to catch up with any of the others; each one hated to have to admit that he'd gone down in defeat. And Eelka was too slow and far behind and full of breakfast to make the effort.

It had been a scheme, hatched and planned after church yesterday. That was what Pier and Dirk had said to do about fathers—pester them until they gave in. If all the children worked at it, nagged and pleaded . . . Oh, your father would growl and act angry and make wisecracks, but that's the way men are, different from mothers. You didn't get to know your father very well—always out at sea—but that's the way it had to be done. Joke a little and tease and nag, and nag and tease. Wait and see! In spite of what your father said or growled, sooner or later he'd do what you wanted.

Some of the others had had their misgivings, Eelka especially. He'd said that *his* father would say, 'Oh, sure, Eelka,' and then not do it. But Pier and Dirk had knowingly assured them all that it was much easier than with mothers. You'd get a sound box on the ear from your mother if you kept on pestering her like that. But then your mother had you yapping around her all the time so she had less patience.

The others, all but Eelka, had been easily convinced, especially since the success of the scheme meant that not only would the wheel be put up on the school, but they'd also have the rest of the day free from lessons. It was worth a good try. But Eelka had

155

said his father was just too good-natured; he wouldn't be pestered.

The scheme had failed miserably. Now each child on his way to school hated to admit to the others that he had failed, not knowing that the others had failed just as completely.

The storm was never going to stop. They knew it! There wouldn't be a stork left after this storm. Everything was hopeless and useless. Even if there should be one or two storks left over from the storm, what was the good of that? There'd be no wheel on the school anyway—just because of their fathers.

They had to face each other in the porch of the school. It was cold in the porch, but at least here they were sheltered from the vicious wind. They all made great pretence of blowing and stamping and beating their arms; they all breathed heavily. 'Whew, what a wind!' somebody said. The others said nothing. They eyed each other while they flailed their arms across their chests in a great pretence of cold and chill.

Finally Jella turned on Dirk and Pier as the authors of the scheme. 'Well,' he demanded, 'is your dad coming?'

Pier and Dirk looked at each other. 'No-oo,' Pier admitted slowly.

That cleared the air. 'Mine isn't either. You should have heard him!'

'Neither is mine. He isn't coming at all. Said he'd just as soon try to sail the sea in a bushel basket in this storm as sit on the sharp roof of this school. Now maybe—he said—if we had a saddle, he might try it. But what good was a fisherman split in two on the ridge of a sharp roof in a high wind? The two halves of him—he didn't think—could go out fishing afterwards and catch double the amount of fish.'

In spite of themselves they all laughed at the sally.

Now that they'd all admitted failure, they tried to outdo each other in repeating what their fathers had said. Now they could laugh about it. And Eelka didn't say, 'What did I tell you?' He was laughing too hard.

Jella summed it up for all of them. 'Perhaps it *is* too windy for old men like our dads.'

The teacher suddenly stood in the doorway.

Lina burst out with it for the group. 'None of our fathers—not a single one—would come,' she said. 'Not a one would get from behind the stove. There they sit, baking!'

'So,' the teacher said. 'So is that the grievance? Wise men, I'd say. You'll have to learn that, too, sooner or later, you can't defy a storm—that you can't hurt a wall with just your head. So let's go inside; let's start right in on our lessons to get our minds on other things. Your fathers will come through. You know that. If not today, the first possible day that the storm will let them. They'll put up the wheel before they set out to sea again.'

'Did they tell you that?' Lina asked eagerly.

'No, they didn't tell me. I know that. And all of you ought to know it, too. Fathers always come through when it's possible. It's the way of fathers and mothers. You're just impatient, but the wheel can wait now. The storks will be waiting out the storm. Let's be just as patient and wise as the storks.'

The lessons didn't go too well in spite of the teacher's reassurances. The wind, howling and shrieking around the corners of the exposed school, kept reminding them of the storm sweeping across the sea and the land. The wagon wheel leaning against the blackboard kept reminding them of storks. The howl of the wind made it difficult to understand the teacher and made it even more difficult to concentrate on answers. Who could think out arithmetic problems when hundreds of storks coming from Africa were maybe going down in the sea? How many storks would drown and never come to Shora? That was the outrageous arithmetic problem the wind seemed to be howling at them.

The teacher asked Auka how much sixteen times sixteen were. Auka had to jerk his attention away from the window where a tuft of hay was held against the glass by the relentless wind. 'There won't be a single stork can come through a storm like this,' Auka answered.

Nobody smiled at Auka's mistake. All eyes went anxiously to the window and from the window to the huge wagon wheel leaning against the front blackboard. Even the teacher looked sombre.

'It's getting still worse,' somebody in a back seat muttered.

'It only seems that way,' the teacher said slowly, 'because we feel so helpless. Because we're just sitting still and doing nothing about the wheel. Inaction is hard, and still, Auka, the only problem before us that we can do anything about is: How much are sixteen times sixteen?'

There was a long pause. Auka had to jerk his mind from his own inside woes, and then work out the answer. He got it wrong.

'Oh,' he said moodily to himself, 'I thought he said sixteen times eighteen.'

Nobody but Auka cared that his answer was wrong. Not even the teacher! The teacher himself was standing listening to the sounds outside. The wind seemed to be making new noises. Muttering, grumbling noises penetrated the classroom door. Outside the porch there was a sound as of something crashing down. Now there were stumbling noises in the porch. The wind must have blown something in and was rolling it around.

Everybody's head was cocked toward the classroom door. There came a hard knock. There were voices.

'Our dads!' Lina cried.

The teacher hurried to open the door. There stood the men of Shora. 'It isn't sane. It's insane,' one of the men said to the teacher. It sounded like Eelka's father. 'First the kids nag you every waking minute, so you chase the kids off to school. What happens then? Their mothers start in on you! Nobody's got anything on the brain but those dratted storks on that wagon wheel. Well, they nagged us all out of our houses, so we got together and decided it was less grief putting up that wheel than facing a bunch of nagging women and children.'

The teacher grinned at the men. 'Solomon found that out a few thousand years before you. Didn't he in his Proverbs say that it was better to sit on the roof of a house than with a nagging woman inside the house?'

Auka's father turned to the men behind him. 'Did you hear that? If his wives had even wise old Solomon up on a roof, what are a few simple fishermen going to do?'

'Get on the roof with Solomon,' somebody said in the porch. 'He knew when he was licked.'

The schoolroom tittered. The men were joking, and, in spite of the storm, they were going to try to put the wheel up. And they weren't unhappy about it —you could tell that—not if they were making wise-cracks. That was always a good sign.

Jella's hefty father peered over the head of the teacher into the classroom. 'It seems I was told,' he boomed, 'that part of the deal was that if we put that wheel on the roof, there'd be no school today. Was I correctly informed, or was that just Jella and his end-less love for school?'

'No-oo,' the whole room sang out. 'No school. *He* promised!'

159

They did not wait for the teacher so much as to nod his head; they could see it in his face—anything went today. They streamed from the room and got into jackets and stocking caps and wooden shoes.

From the porch they saw that their fathers had even brought ladders and timber and ropes. The stuff lay in a helter-skelter pile in the playground where it had been dropped.

'Out of the way! Out of the way, all you mortals,' Jella came shouting. Jella alone had remembered. He had jumped to the front of the room to get the wagon wheel instead of just rushing out with the rest. Now he sent the wheel rolling wildly into the porch. Everybody had to scatter. The wheel wobbled in an uncertain path, somehow found the outside doorway, plunged outside, and settled itself on the pile of beams and ropes and ladders.

'Well, it's all here now,' a man shouted. 'Now roll out your storks.'

The men laughed, but not the children. Happy and relieved and eager as they were, now that their fathers

were actually going to put up the wheel, it was not a good joke. The low, sweeping sky, scudding and racing with clouds that looked as angry as capped waves on the sea, threatened bad things. There was nothing in the sky but storm, there wasn't a bird anywhere, not even a sparrow. A rain squall slashed down. The wind hurled the rain into the porch.

'Will there be any storks left after a storm like this?' Dirk asked the group of men around the pile in the playground.

The men looked up at the sky and shrugged. 'Maybe, if the storm doesn't hang on too long,' Lina's father said. 'Maybe a couple of them will have sense enough to bury their heads in sand until this blows over.'

'That's ostriches!' Lina, standing right beside him, said scornfully. She was half-ashamed of the ignorance of her father—and right before the teacher! 'Ostriches are *supposed* to bury their heads in the sand, only they don't.'

'I think that settles you and your ostriches,' Eelka's father said.

'All right,' Lina's father said, nettled. 'I'd better go and bury my head in some sand. These modern-day school kids—they know everything, don't they? Me, all I know is fish.' He grinned suddenly. 'You kids wouldn't be satisfied with a couple of fish on the roof?' he asked plaintively. 'Say a couple of sharks in a wash tub?'

The children hooted, and he grinned broadly. He sobered, stepped back, and eyed the sharp school roof. 'Well, come on, you Solomons,' he said impatiently. 'Let's get on the roof and get that wheel up.'

The men stood studying the steep roof. 'Wet and steep and windy, it'll be slipperier than a deckful of jellyfish,' one of them said. 'But up with a ladder, and we'll see what the climate is up there.'

Two men raised the long ladder high and straight. As they carried it upright around a corner of the school, a blast of wind caught the high ladder. The two men struggled, but they couldn't hold it up. The ladder swayed and twisted and threatened to come crashing down.

Everybody stood anxiously watching the top of the ladder, expecting it to smash to pieces against the ground at any moment. 'Watch it. Watch it,' somebody yelled. 'If you can't even set a ladder up, how do you expect to get a wheel up there? Get into it all of you; don't stand there staring at the top rung. Let it down! Let it down, I say. There. Now carry it flat around that windy corner. That isn't a flag you're carrying in a parade.'

It was Janus! There he came in his wheel chair, forcing it ahead against the wind by sheer strength and at the same time loudly scolding everybody.

The men let the ladder down. Then they turned to face Janus, a bit peeved at being scolded before their own children. But Janus was grinning broadly; he was having a fine time in spite of the wind and the struggle to move against it. He rolled up to the group in his wheel chair. 'When it comes to doing anything on land, you lot are about as helpless as the fish are,' he told them. He turned his chair so as to face the roof. 'Now then, let's use our heads. Better yet, I'll use my head.'

'So now we've got an overseer,' one of the men said.

'All right, now lay that ladder down,' Janus directed. 'Place one end against the wall, then raise the other end. Get under it; walk your hands from spoke to spoke until it's up straight against the wall. Then all you have to do is pull out the bottom end. See, that way you don't fight the wind.'

'Well, that worked,' one of the men said.

When the ladder was up, the men automatically

turned to Janus for further instruction. Janus looked at the pile of timber and the one ladder beside it.

'Now the other ladder and push it up on the roof. But first tie a coil of rope on the top rung, and then let the rope down the other side of the roof to fasten the ladder down. Then lash the second ladder to the first, otherwise the wind will just sweep it right off the roof. Meanwhile, you kids get me that wagon wheel.'

While he waited for the children to roll the big wheel to him, Janus kept looking at the pile of beams and boards still lying in the schoolyard. 'What's the big pile for?' he yelled up to the roof.

'To brace up the wheel. Got to have some brackets or braces or something to hold the wheel on the sharp ridge of this roof,' Auka's father explained.

'Yes, but you're just going to have storks up there, not elephants,' Janus said scornfully. 'The way I've planned it—that wheel's got to be up there nice and simple. With all your beams and boards and two-by-fours sticking in every direction, storks flying overhead will think it's a trap, not a nest. But just get on with that ladder, Janus will fix it nice and neat and simple.'

'Yes, sir, yes, sir,' Auka's father said. 'Up with the second ladder, men, Janus says.'

Jella, Auka, and Lina rolled the wagon wheel before Janus. 'Now where's that saw?' Janus said impatiently. 'Somewhere I hung a saw on this wheel chair contraption.'

'There it is,' Pier said behind him. 'You brought a hammer, too. You're sitting on it.'

'The hammer, too,' Janus said. 'The hammer first.' Then paying no attention to the alarmed looks of the children, he took the hammer and drove the steel rim off the inner wooden rim of the wheel. After studying the pitch of the roof and the ridge, he began sawing a deep V into the side of the wooden rim. The children had to hold the wheel steady for him while he sawed. 'See, I'll cut two deep V's; that way the rim will fit snug on the ridge,' he explained. 'Then we'll fit the iron rim just partly over the wooden one, so that it won't cover the V notches. The iron doesn't have to cover the whole wooden rim—this wheel isn't going rolling any more—it'll even be better that way. With the iron rim sticking up, it'll make a sort of pan of the wheel—storks are awfully sloppy nest builders. This may help them to hold all the stuff they'll lug up on this wheel.'

The teacher came up. 'Janus, don't you want to go inside? No sense in your sitting here in the wind when you can do your work just as well inside.'

'If those men can sit on that windy roof, I can sit here where it's practically cosy,' Janus said shortly, his whole grim attention on his sawing.

The teacher, realizing Janus wanted no favours, said no more. 'Anything I can do?' he asked. 'I feel rather useless with everybody else busy.'

'Well, I need a brace and bit—a long bit to go through the ridge boards on both sides of the roof.'

'My dad's got a brace and all kinds of bits, all sizes,' Jella said eagerly. 'I'll get them.'

'Well, there goes Jella and the job you had for me,' the teacher said.

'Hold it,' Janus said. 'I also need two heavy iron rods—long enough for the two edges of the wheel rim to rest on them. You see, we'll drill the holes through the ridge, shove the rods through them, and then rest the wheel on the rods. The two notches I cut in the wooden rim will fit snugly over the ridge. Then all we'll need to do is to wire the rim to the two supporting rods, and there'll be the wheel, steady and level and solid as a house. But I can't think of anybody in Shora who would have a couple of heavy rods like that.'

164

'Hah!' the teacher said. 'You're talking to the right man. It seems to me I've seen a couple of rods like that in the tower when I go there to ring the bell. I'm almost sure.'

'Make sure they're long enough,' Janus said.

'I'll look, and nobody can take this job away from me. As the official bellringer for the village, I'm the only one to have a key to the tower.' The teacher pulled the big ancient key out of his pocket and held it up. He hurried off.

'Glad I found something for him to do,' Janus said to Lina. 'He makes me nervous watching so closely. He's just as jittery and excited as you kids.' He had finished cutting the notches. Now came the job of fitting the iron rim partially over the wooden rim. The boys and Lina had all they could do to hold the wheel upright and steady as Janus struggled with the close-fitting rim.

Jella returned with the brace and all the bits. A few minutes later the teacher came back with two large, rusty rods. Janus studied the rods. 'They should do. Good and thick and solid. And long enough for the wheel. Good thing you remembered them,' he said to the teacher. 'It must be the only pair of loose rods in Shora. It was the one thing that had me worried—me with my fine plans and no rods. I'd have been the laughing-stock around here.'

Jella was sent up the ladder to carry the brace and bit to his father. The teacher was sent off to find some heavy wire that could be used to secure the wheel to the rods. 'Got to keep him busy,' Janus said with a sly wink at Lina.

At last the wheel was ready. The children rolled it to the ladder. The men began hoisting the huge wagon wheel up the ladder, while Jella's father drilled the two holes for the rods in the ridge of the roof.

It was a slow, hard struggle against the tugging of

165

the wind. Two of the fishermen now straddled the ridge, ready to lift the wheel on to the rods when it reached them. A sudden hard hail and rain squall slashed down again. The men straddling the ridge had to press themselves flat; they lay with faces against the roof and clung with one hand to the ladder. The men working the wheel up the roof had to stop and be content just to hold the wheel in place on the ladder. The squall passed as suddenly as it had come, and the struggle went on again.

Janus watched every move with eagle eyes. He was so intent he seemed unaware of the sweep of wind and rain and hail. Yet from time to time Janus glanced down the road to the village. Suddenly he bellowed out, 'Look at that, men! Look what's coming! The women! What do you think? Wind or hail—here come the women. Pots of hot coffee for you. This is going to turn into a picnic. Hurray for women!'

All work stopped on the roof. Everybody sat looking down the road; they called the women on. The women came in a close group, trying to protect their steaming coffee from the cold wind. Then a new blast of hail had the men hanging on to the roof and the ladders again.

The moment the squall passed, they looked down the road again. 'No use looking,' Janus shouted. 'No hot coffee, no nothing, until that wheel is up and secure.'

'Janus, you're a slave driver,' one of the men on the ridge complained. 'All you need is a whip.'

'Don't need a whip,' Janus called back. 'Got my tongue.'

'Yeah,' Pier and Dirk's father yelled down. 'Too bad that shark didn't get your tongue instead of your legs.'

Down below Janus flushed red and embarrassed. He looked away and then glowered up from under the

166

peak of his cap to see how Pier's father had meant the joke. Pier's father saw the look; he gave Janus a good-natured grin. All of Janus eased in the chair. He let out his breath. 'Well, all I can tell you is,' he called out slowly, 'that shark *was* eyeing my tongue. Got a good look at it, too—all I was telling him! But it looked too tough even for him, I think. He must have decided my sea boots were tenderer. So he took my boots. How could that poor silly fish know my legs were inside of them?'

Everybody laughed, and Janus sat back, relieved. He seemed to test the laugh, almost as if he were tasting it. Then he looked at Pier, hovering anxiously beside his chair. 'Good kid,' he said. 'Don't think I don't know everybody's accepting that crazy story because it's good for me. And it is good!' he added fiercely. 'Good.'

The wheel was being fitted over the ridge. Janus riveted his whole attention on the operation. 'It's got to work, my idea with just two rods,' he muttered anxiously. 'Otherwise my name is mud. They'll laugh me out of Shora.'

The teacher came hurrying up with a handful of wires. Janus picked out the heaviest and sent Pier up the ladder with them. 'Nothing more for you to do,' Janus told the teacher. 'But the women have hot coffee on the stove in the schoolroom. Get yourself a cup. You aren't used to being out in this kind of weather.'

'Aye, aye, sir,' the teacher said. He saluted smartly and trotted off.

Jella's father, lying full-length on the ladder on the roof, was twisting the wire around the rods and the rim of the wheel. It was awkward, slow, overhead work. The cold and the salt, stinging wind were numbing all the men and slowing their movements. The two men straddling the ridge were holding the wheel in place. One of them had to let go his hold to rest his numbed arm. He wearily rubbed a hand over his face to wipe away the icy wetness. He took a new hold, but now the wheel was tilted.

'Jan, hold that wheel straight,' Janus said. 'Those storks need a nest, not a chute.'

'Look,' Jan answered irritably, before he gave a thought to what he was saying, 'if you think you can do it better, you come up here and hold it.'

There was an awkward, stunned pause. Everybody looked at Janus. Lina, beside his chair, laid her hand on Janus's shoulder. But to her astonishment Janus was delighted. 'Did you hear that?' he asked Lina. 'He forgot I've got no legs. Bless his awkward old hide. That's the way it's got to be.'

Now Jan, who had been preoccupied with the wheel and his precarious position, realized what he'd said. He looked down at Janus. A slow grin spread over his face. 'Stay there,' he said. 'I'm not giving you a chance to come up here and show me up. I'll show you I'm as much a man as you are.'

He hadn't apologized or even tried to cover it up. They were treating Janus man to man. He was one of them again. Janus bent low to straighten out the pin in his folded-over trousers leg. He fumbled with it. When he straightened up, his eyes were bright. 'Bless his awkward old hide,' he mumbled.

Lina took her hand off his shoulder. Even she mustn't baby Janus.

'Would you dare?' Janus asked suddenly. 'We've got to test that wheel, and you're the only one who is about the weight of two storks. I've got to know whether it'll hold their nest without tilting or wobbling. The men will hold you up on the wheel.'

Janus wasn't babying her either. 'Sure,' Lina said stoutly.

*   *   *

On the ridge Jan held Lina's hand as she climbed on the wheel. Janus directed from down below. Lina walked along the rim of the wheel as far as Jan could reach and still keep his hold on her. Janus watched her closely. 'You can come down now,' he said. 'It'll hold. It didn't so much as stir, even with you walking on the edge. Everybody down now! Take the ropes and ladders down and go and get your coffee.'

Lina made use of that moment of distraction to pull free from Jan's hand. She climbed up on the hub of the wheel. She flapped her arms. 'I'm a stork, I'm a stork,' she cried. The next moment a gust of wind caught her, and she had to let herself fall, clutching for the spokes of the wheel and grabbing wildly for Jan's outstretched hand. She hung on for dear life.

'Some stork!' the boys jeered up at her. 'Let's see you fly down.'

'Jan, come on down and bring that stork with you under your arms,' Janus said, 'before she tries to fly. I wouldn't put it past her.'

It was a picnic—steaming coffee and cakes and doughnuts. It was a feast! Hot chocolate milk for the boys and Lina! That was what made it really a picnic and a feast. You had hot chocolate milk only on the Queen's Birthday and doughnuts only on Santa Claus Day. But now doughnuts and chocolate all the same day! And the rest of the day free—it was a holiday.

The school room buzzed. Janus was in the midst of it in his wheel chair. His voice carried above all the others. But everybody was in high spirits. They'd wrestled the wheel up on the roof in spite of storm and cold and hail and squalls. It made it a holiday.

No school the rest of the day, and their fathers home with games to play. They'd all play dominoes with their dads. The five boys and Lina decided it among themselves as they sat in their seats, sipping hot chocolate while the grown-ups crowded around the warm stove.

It happened so seldom, having their fathers home. Always they were out at sea or, if home, busy with nets and sails and the readying of the boats. Now they'd have almost a whole day with their dads. The storm had made it a holiday for them, a chance for games and jokes with their fathers.

Everybody was talking, and Janus was in the midst of everything. Now he noticed the boys and Lina in their corner. 'How is it?' he asked. 'Is this a feast or isn't it?'

'Hot chocolate milk and hot doughnuts!' Pier told him smartly. 'Hey, Janus, all it lacks is some cherries.'

Janus laughed. 'To get them you'd have to go where the wind took them—over a couple of provinces or so, I think, or maybe into Germany. Well, there're a few under the tree, if you like salt cherries.'

Lina hastily told the boys that she was going to ask Janus to play dominoes, too. He and Jana had no children. Janus ought to be invited, too. They all agreed eagerly; they all wanted Janus in their houses.

'Oh, no, you don't,' Lina said. 'I thought of it first!'

CHAPTER XIII

Flotsam
and Jetsam

THE storm lasted three more days. Behind the dike the ebb tide struggled against the might of the wind in the great elementary need of a tide to obey its laws. But the wind won and held the tidewater to the shore. Even in ebb tide the sea lashed angry and deep. Great waves roared and stormed halfway up the straining dike. Over the houses and village the wind shrieked. It screamed along the tiles on the roofs, and often it loosened tiles and sent them crashing. Already several windows had been broken by flying roof tiles, and the blinds of the houses in Shora were kept shut throughout the storm days to protect the windows.

Inside the cluttered little houses the fishermen fretted at the delay and the confinement. For five days now each fisherman had been cooped up in his little house—one living room, a hall, and a kitchen. The living room, with its bedding from the box beds piled over every chair, seemed always to be in the long, awkward process of bedmaking. The restless fishermen were growing irritated by the closeness of the dark,

171

shut-up houses, the smell of their own stale tobacco smoke, the babies and little children that seemed always to be underfoot.

The older children could be got out of the way by sending them to school, but there, it seemed to the irritated fishermen, they did little but agonize about the storm and what it would do to the storks. Mighty little book knowledge was being rammed into their worried heads these miserable, nerve-racking days. The men were getting as fed up with talk of storks as they were with playing dominoes.

On the fifth day of the storm Lina's father finally swept the whole mess of dominoes off the table so hard that two of them landed in the ash box of the peat stove that his wife was just emptying. 'You can't eat dominoes,' he exploded. 'It seems when I'm not holding a half-wet tot, I'm keeping older kids quiet with dominoes. Dominoes! It's getting so that I've spots before my eyes!' He grabbed his oiled coat and charged to the door. 'I'm readying the boat. By tomorrow this should be over. There's a new note to the wind.' He looked at his wife, who was trying to extract the two dominoes from the hot ashes into which they had sunk. 'Oh, I know I'm the clutter here. Me and my long legs need a sea.'

All the fishermen seemed to have reached breaking point at about the same time. Men came striding from different little houses. The others, hearing their voices in the street, hurried out after them. On the dike they got busy with nets and gear, in spite of the struggle and double work in the storm. They worked, yelling at each other against the wind, and the wind carried the sounds into the houses. It was good to hear busy sounds outside again. The women breathed more easily and started cleaning the impossible rooms.

'Maybe tomorrow we can open doors and windows and let in air,' Lina's mother said hopefully. 'Who knows—maybe even sunshine! It'd be so good to see the sun again.'

It had to wait. Even the fishermen had to give the sea and storm another night. If there were a new tone to the wind and if the storm were flagging, as the fishermen insisted, the sea did not seem to know it. As if by habit, it lashed on and churned and raged behind the dike. But toward night there was the slightest veering of the north wind, so slight it could be noticed only by a fisherman.

The fishermen stood on the dike in a solemn group, sensing the wind change, studying the scudding, angry clouds, almost tasting the change in the salty spray that the sea hurled up at them. To them it all spelled the change—the going-out to sea again. They'd be ready to go in the morning, no matter if the sea had not yet reacted to the coming change. They knew the storm was broken; the sea would settle down in time.

Fortunately, it being Thursday, this was the day of the arrival of the newspaper, a two-page, closely printed weekly sheet, that brought news of the rest of the country and of far lands. Only one copy of the newspaper came to the fishermen of Shora. It passed from hand to hand until the village had literally read it to pieces. No dominoes this long evening! A man had to read the paper when it came—thoroughly, completely, down to the last inky word. But fast! Somebody else was waiting for it.

The men read it out loud that Thursday evening so that busy wives and older children could share in it at one and the same time. They watched the clock as they read; by such an hour it had to be carried to the house next door.

The reading of the paper was dull stuff for the children. Dominoes was more fun, but grown-ups tired so soon of games.

Now there was little to do but play with the dominoes all by yourself—set them up on end in a long file, like soldiers, then topple the first one, and watch them all topple in turn. That way you did some good, too. It kept the younger children interested and quiet so that they didn't interrupt the all-important, almost sacred reading of the newspaper, full of the dull doings of parliaments and ministers and foreign diplomats in strange countries with strange, faraway-sounding names.

Auka sat listening to his father's reading. His father held up the paper to point out an unpronounceable word to Auka's mother. Auka glanced at the paper. Suddenly his attention froze on the word *Africa*. It seemed to leap out at him from among all the other words in the column. He forgot to push down the dominoes he had set up in a curving row for his little brother, Jan. He read:

> It is thought that the five-day violent storm raging over the country and all western Europe will have done unaccountable harm to the influx of storks from Africa. The storm came at the height of the migration. It is feared that all the storks winging their way over seas when the storm broke may have perished. We in Holland can expect most of our nesting places on barns and roofs and in the stork rookeries to remain empty this year. The situation is the more tragic in that of recent years the stork population was beginning to show some gains again. It is estimated that this will set them back for years to come.

Auka had read, now he sat still as if spelling out to himself the meaning of the stilted, heavy words. It was hard to believe, but there it stood in print in the paper. One thing made it horribly believable though —his father had skipped the item about the storks when he had read that page of the paper out loud.

'Push 'em,' Auka's little brother, Jan, pleaded, his eyes on the curving row of dominoes marching across the table. 'Push 'em, Auka!'

174

Auka pushed them, then he slipped from behind the table. 'I've got to see Pier and Dirk a minute,' he said.

His mother looked up. 'Now in the storm and rain?' she asked mildly, but she had her mind on what Auka's father was reading. Auka drew on a jacket; bare-headed, he dashed into the rain-swept street.

Nobody knew! In every house where the paper had already been read, the news of the storks perishing in the storm had been kept silent. That made it all seem worse. Lina joined Auka and Dirk and Pier; they went on to Jella's house, then to Eelka's. Everybody had to know.

But what was there to do? It was in the newspaper so it was to be believed. It was news, it was a fact. There was nothing they could do—it was the storm. God brought storms and hurled big storks into the ocean to become food for fish. They sat stunned in Eelka's kitchen.

'But some will get through,' Lina said desperately. She was begging for them to agree rather than just stating a fact.

'Yes, but those have gone to all the old places. You know what Janus said. Only the new storks from last year would look for new places like our school to nest. Janus told us on Sunday in church that it was the young storks that still had to come, and it's those that went down in the sea.'

'I wonder if Janus knows? And the teacher?'

'Oh, the teacher would know.'

'Maybe we ought to tell Janus . . . Let's go and tell Janus.'

'But could we all go there?' Jella asked doubtfully. 'All us kids? We've never been.'

But they had to do something. They couldn't sit still.

*　　　*　　　*

Jana came to the door and let the children stand outside in the rain and wind. 'Will you tell Janus the storks are all down?' Pier asked sombrely.

'Are those the kids?' Janus shouted from inside the house. 'Well, bring them in. I sort of thought they'd come after that newspaper story.'

They trooped in in single file. The boys ripped their caps off and fussed with unbuttoning jackets. So Lina had to take the lead behind Jana down the hall into the kitchen where Janus sat drinking a cup of hot chocolate milk. 'Pour some more water into the chocolate milk, and we'll all have a cup,' he told Jana.

Janus was joking! Even after that awful news in the paper, he sat there joking and sipping chocolate milk! The children, even Pier, found nothing to say.

'Janus, did you read what it said in the paper?' Lina asked at last. Her voice quavered.

Then Janus blew up. 'Read it? Sure, I read it—read it so many times I know it by heart. But don't you kids stand there and tell me that you took that silly scribbling to heart! There he sits, that inky printer in a cellar somewhere in Amsterdam; buildings all around so high he can't even see as much as a square foot of sky. He and his inky fingers in his cellar!'

Janus drew indignant breath. 'Why, I'll bet you he couldn't even tell a stork from a rooster. Storks don't settle in cities. But he knows! Even knows that all the storks drowned in the sea. Was he out in a boat in the storm? Did he see them fall in the sea? Did he see stork bodies wash up against the dike?

'No, he didn't!' Janus fiercely answered himself. 'He had a pailful of ink to get rid of, and he had to fill his paper with words. There was a little blank spot he still had to fill, so he put something about storks in that left-over space. Anything he could think up. "It is thought. It is feared. It is estimated!" ' he quoted derisively from the newspaper.

'Who thinks it? Who fears it? The printer! Words! All fancy words to worry kids in Shora with!' Janus glared at them all. He looked at his big hands. If the hateful printer that Janus had imagined had been there, it would have gone hard with him and his inky neck.

'Did any of you see stork bodies wash up on the dike?' Janus asked.

'No,' Lina said. 'No, but then we didn't look, either.'

It was absolutely the wrong answer. Janus looked at Lina as if she were the hateful printer. 'Printers! Ink! Words!' Janus snorted. 'Look, those storks make that trip twice a year. Look, if that printer came out of his cellar and went to sea in a boat in a storm, he'd go down before he got ten feet from the dike. But your fathers don't go down, do they? They bring a boat through—they know about storms. Well, so do storks! Sure, a few may go down, but those storks just don't fold their wings and let themselves be dumped in the sea to become fish bait. They're too smart to let themselves be caught over water in a storm. They knew in their bones, long before the storm fell, that a storm was coming. And they didn't have to read about it in any printer's silly newspaper!'

Janus had made the contest of wits between the wise storks and the stupid printer so vivid, it seemed real. He quieted down now as Jana passed out cups of steaming chocolate milk. 'No, you'll see, the storm will hold them up for a few days. The storm will have scattered them. But in a couple of days, you can start looking in the sky for storks again. They'll be coming just by twos, not by flights, because they let the storm take them over the land wherever it wanted—but not down in the sea! They'll come through, all but maybe a few foolish young storks, making their first trip back.'

'But you said on Sunday, Janus, that those were just the ones we need here in Shora,' Jella said anxiously. 'You said young ones would look for a new place like Shora. The old ones will just go back to their old places.'

'But that's just it, you young fathead,' Janus shouted impatiently. 'Don't you see? The storm is going to help us, because it scattered the storks. Some that otherwise would go to Germany will land here in our province of Friesland. And the storm will have held them up almost a week. They can't fool around looking for the old places hundreds of miles from where they've been blown. They're going to take what they can get, the first wheel they see.'

Over their cups the children's eyes stayed hopefully on Janus. He was so sure; if anything, he was even surer than that printer in his newspaper. And Janus did not live in a cellar. For years Janus had sat in a wheel chair doing nothing but watching birds. Janus knew. And before that, Janus had been a fisherman; he knew about the sea and storms, too.

'The wind's been blowing all these days straight out of the sea,' Eelka said slowly. 'Even if the storks had been over the sea, they'd be blown away over the land, wouldn't they, Janus?' Eelka had thought it all out.

All of a sudden the chocolate milk started tasting much better. It was delicious. Janus took a long sip himself. 'Now that's thinking,' he said to Eelka. 'And that's the way it is. That's thinking it out; it isn't just printing words in a paper. "It is thought, it is feared, it is estimated!" ' It made him angry all over again; he snorted into his cup so hard it made bubbles.

'Another pailful of water into that chocolate milk, Mother,' he told Jana. 'We all need another cup to settle our nerves—that newspaper!'

It suddenly felt chummy and cosy in the kitchen. At the stove Jana made a little joke, and everybody

laughed. The children looked at each other and took sips of the delicious chocolate milk. Oh, it was good to sit here with Janus after the awful scare.

Janus waited for them to finish drinking their chocolate milk. 'Now,' he said. 'Now I want you to come and take a look in the living room.'

'Oh, no, Janus!' Jana protested. 'What'll they think?'

'They're kids,' Janus said. 'Not fussy housewives. Come on, everybody.'

They filed into Janus's living room. There on the table lay Eelka's wheel! It was all fitted together except for the iron rim that had sunk to the bottom of the canal. The whole floor was littered with rusty tin scraps and wood chips and shavings. The room was a mess, but the amazed children had eyes only for the big ancient wagon wheel on the table. Janus had begun to fit pieces of rusted tin around the outside of the wooden rim, all the sections of which had been glued and nailed together. The spokes were all in place; the big hub rose high in the centre of the living room table.

'Now what do you think?' Janus asked proudly. 'Do you think I'd go to all that fuss if I didn't expect storks? Ripped the rope out of the cherry tree and used the tin that had been on it. The tin will hold the wooden rim together, and it's rusty enough so it won't blink and shine and scare storks. A few more pieces of tin to lap and nail around the rim, another night for the glue to dry, and up she goes on Janus's roof. That's if it's all right with you, Eelka?'

'Oh, golly,' Eelka said.

Lina's eyes shone. 'But that's what the teacher said —if only we'd start. Now look there's already a second wheel for a second roof. Who knows? Maybe some day there'll be a wheel on every roof in Shora.'

'And trees,' Auka said. 'We're going to plant trees, too.'

'But where are we ever going to find more wheels?' Jella said. 'It'll take years.'

'Years, my eye!' Janus said. 'I've got it all doped out, kids. I can *make* wheels. All I need is wood, and that the sea will bring us after every storm.'

'Yes, Janus,' Pier said eagerly. 'We'll hunt all along the dike from here to Ternaad, even. Douwa can tell us whenever he sees a good piece of driftwood on his walks, and we'll bring it in.'

'I'll shape it into some kind of a wheel,' Janus promised. 'So long as it has bars across—like the spokes on a wagon wheel—for the storks to build a nest on. So long as it's sturdy enough to hold a couple, storks aren't fussy. And all I'll need is wood and tin, and it gives me something to do.'

'Oh, and after this storm there'll be all kinds of driftwood,' Eelka said. 'We'll pile your yard full, we'll bring it wherever you want it, Janus,' he promised eagerly.

'But not in my living room!' Jana said from the doorway. 'I've a hard enough time keeping it decent after peddling bread all day. You're not making a wheel factory out of my living room and filling it full of wet, scummy flotsam and jetsam out of the sea.'

'The shed in the yard will be our factory,' Janus decided on the moment. 'Hey, we'll need a sign: "Wheel Factory of the Shora Wheel and Stork Society," or something.'

'The Shora Wheel and Stork Society,' Lina cried. 'Janus, that's good! Why, that's us—that's what we'll be. The next wheel has to go on Grandmother Sibble III's house, and the next one on Douwa's, and then we'll toss up to see which one of us gets the next wheel. And Janus will be the president! And the teacher the vice-president, and . . .'

'No,' Jana said. 'I'm the vice-president right now, and right now this meeting is adjourned, else all your mothers will think you perished in the night and the storm. Away with you, and give me a chance to straighten up this room.'

'It seems that we get no vote in the matter,' Janus said. 'Night, kids.'

'Good night, Janus!'

Thoughtful, and excited, the Shora Wheel and Stork Society filed meekly out of the house.

CHAPTER XIV

The Tots
in the Tower

IN THE morning the storm was over, that is, well enough over for the fishermen to go out in the early hours to test the swirling, lashing sea. All Shora was astir. Although it was two o'clock in the morning, there was a light in every window. The fishermen were taking no chances—the ebb tide was due at four o'clock. If the storm was no longer strong enough to hold the ebb tide water to the dike, their anchored boats would be left high and dry.

The wind still blew. The sea still stormed against the dike. But the sound of voices and the clatter of wooden shoes was in the street. Doors slammed. Shouts came from the dike. It was the last-minute excitement of casting off for sea. Wives would not see their husbands again for weeks, while the men in their little fishing boats would be out on the treacherous North Sea.

The fishermen wouldn't wait for the storm to calm down still more. 'If we'd wait for every two-cent storm, we'd always be sitting on the dike,' Jella's father shouted as a farewell when the dinghy left his fishing boat to return to the dike. Three women rowed it back. This time the dinghy had to be left behind. The sea was too roiled to risk hoisting it on board the boat of Jella's father to serve as a lifeboat for the little fishing fleet.

The children had slept through all the turmoil of the preparation and departure. They woke up at their usual schooltime to find that their homes and the village had gone back to the normal pattern of life—no fathers, just mothers and their children. It seemed very natural. Things were back in their groove. But this morning the departure of the fishermen signified one added and important thing, the end to the storm.

Clothes hastily thrown on, breakfasts gulped, all the children instinctively did the same thing. Before setting out for school, they raced to the top of the high dike. There they found each other, and there they stood dismayed. The sea still lashed, the waves still leaped.

After their first disappointment, the little group on the dike realized there was a difference. As the children of fishermen, they sensed it. The fishing fleet was long since out of sight. It must be far beyond the islands that now appeared as dark masses in the distance and then fell back into the tossing sea again. An old black steamer wallowed and plunged this side of the islands. But here against the dike the waves were not washing quite so high. The thin licks of the breakers did not hiss and boil as fearfully up the slope of the dike as they had yesterday.

The eyes of all the children went to the high scudding clouds far away over the sea. Out there under the clouds, halfway to the plunging steamer, a sea eagle was rising and falling on windy currents of air. A sea eagle! A bird! But where were the gulls? The seashore without gulls seemed wrong. Maybe a sea eagle could ride the rough winds, but the gulls had not yet returned. The storm had taken them far inland!

Then the children heard the great bronze bell in the village tower. It was eight o'clock. The schoolteacher was ringing the bell. It was summoning the farm workers round about Shora home for breakfast. It was the end of their first four-hour shift.

Even the bell sounded different this morning. Under the wind the peals of the bell sounded solemn and sweet as they lilted over the dike. The children listened. 'The storm is over, is almost over.' The bell seemed to sing the powerful song with a great promise of hopeful, sunshiny days to come—of great things ahead.

But the boys and Lina could stay no longer on the dike. Now it was schooltime. They were supposed to be at the door of the school when the teacher returned from ringing the tower bell that called the workers home from the fields. The children raced each other down the dike. The clouds scudded far overhead, but the children of Shora laughed and shouted in the street as they raced each other to school.

The teacher left the heavy iron door at the foot of the tower wide-open. He didn't have to close it now against the raw gusts of salty wind and the spray that had leaped the dike these many days. He tugged at the bell rope and looked out of the open door. The crisp, clean look of the wind-swept village square held his attention. The storm was going over; the air was fresh again. He rang the bell harder. The great tower filled with the solemn hum of the bell. He stopped at last. Slowly the echoes of the bell seeped out of the big stone room. Then the tower was silent except for the loud ticking of the huge clock in a loft far above him.

The teacher stood listening to the ticking of the clock. To his expert ear the sound was not right, a little off-beat. He bit his lower lip in vexation, remembering that he hadn't wound the clock all the days of the storm. He realized he had let it go too long. If he didn't climb up now and wind the clock, it would stop in an hour or so. He looked out of the door. The children were gone from the dike. They'd be waiting for him at the school. Well, they'd have to wait a little longer while he climbed to the loft and wound the clock—waiting for school to open must be one thing a child could be patient about, maybe the only thing.

The teacher started climbing the first long ladder. As he crossed over the floor of the first loft to the next ladder, he heard the voices of children in the square below the tower, the smaller children, with tiny shrill voices. The mothers must have got the small fry out of the house almost as soon as the school children.

Down below, the teacher had left the iron door to the tower wide-open. The gate to the churchyard around the tower stood open.

Linda, Lina's little sister, had found Jan, Auka's little brother. Jan was her special little playmate. Linda had a great plan. She and Jan were going to make a daisy chain. She had seen her sister, Lina, do it. It was easy. Other small children were playing in the village square before the churchyard. They wanted Linda and Jan to come, but Linda and Jan were going to make a daisy chain. Jan didn't know what a daisy chain was, but Linda would show him. 'Come on, Jan.' She went through the gate into the churchyard. She had never been there alone before, always the gate was closed. Somehow what she was doing seemed forbidden, a little bit wrong. 'Come on, Jan.'

Jan obediently followed her through the gate. They found two daisies behind the first gravestone and crouched down to pick them. Hidden by the stone, they were immediately forgotten by the other little

185

children in the square in the excitement of their own play. Linda found three more half-opened daisies. They wandered on toward the tower.

Jan was the first to see that the tower door stood wide-open. It intrigued him. It was much more interesting than daisies, and they needed, oh, a hundred, Linda had said. Jan had no idea what a hundred was, but it sounded like a pailful. Jan tiptoed into the tower. Immediately the silence and the gloom of the cold, ancient, stone room frightened him. He ran out. 'Come on, Linda. Look in here. Oh, it's big!' With five daisies clutched in her hand, Linda came. Side by side, they went into the tower.

They stopped before the bell rope, awed and a little scared. But the outer door stood wide-open and there was light from the doorway. The comforting sounds of the other children, playing in the windy square, came to them. Along one side of the stone room was a cage with bars. It intrigued Linda.

There was an old bare cot at the back of the cage. It was suspended from the wall by two heavy chains. Suddenly Linda remembered—this was the jail where they put bad men! She told Jan. They both breathed heavily. But outside, the other children were yelling nice and loud, and through the open door they could see the dike.

'Sometimes when I'm very bad my mother says that she's going to put me in there,' Jan whispered. 'She won't though, will she?'

'Oh, no!' Linda assured him, her lips quivering. She knew the same threat only too well.

They retreated farther from the bars. There was a noise above them. Linda looked toward it. Up the shaft of dim light with the many ladders going up in the tower, Linda saw legs coming down a ladder.

'Look, Jan.'

Now footsteps were right overhead. A little dust

sifted down in their upturned faces. Then the legs were thrust through the trap door opening into the big stone room. Breathlessly Linda pulled Jan behind the big iron door. He was so slow. It was the teacher up there! The teacher of Lina and all the older boys was coming down the ladder—an awesome man, high and mighty, and scary to a little girl who did not go to school. Linda put her hand over Jan's mouth. He was so silly—he might say things.

The door behind which they were hiding pulled away from in front of them. It clanged shut. A key grated in the lock. There was no other sound; there was darkness except for a small feeble square of light filtering down from the higher lofts in the tower. It fell on the bars of the cage. They were locked in the tower, in the dark stone room with the jail for big, bad men. And the teacher was gone. Jan began to cry. Linda, almost crying herself, tried to comfort him.

Jan pushed her away. 'I want my mother,' he wailed.

That unnerved Linda. Just then there was nothing in all the world that she wanted more than *her* mother. The light filtered down on the bars of the cell. Linda stared at them with big eyes. She swallowed the beginning of a sob. 'Let's climb up,' she urged. 'Oh, we can see everything from up there, the houses, and even the islands in the sea!' She promised Jan all the good things she could think of, because she was promising them to herself. She was afraid of the cell and the bars, but she couldn't tell Jan that. Up there in the tower it was light, up there there wouldn't be a cage.

Jan did not want to climb; he wanted his mother. Linda pushed him toward the ladder. 'I'll climb right up behind you, then you can't fall,' she told him. She kept her eyes turned away from the bars and almost lifted Jan up on the ladder. Jan had to concentrate on spanning the space from rung to rung with his short, fat legs. He couldn't concentrate and cry and want his mother all at the same time—he climbed. Little sobs still came pushing out of him with the effort, but Linda crowded on behind him to get away from the cell and bars behind her in the dark room.

The children climbed toward the light. When at last they pulled themselves through the trap door opening, there was just a loft with another long rickety ladder. But here there was light. The light streamed through a windowlike opening far too high for them to look out. But here there was no cell with bars.

They held hands, awed by the stillness and the strangeness of the place. Through the high opening no sound came—no sound now of other children playing in the square. The world and the village seemed far away and gone. They looked at the ladder leading to the next higher loft.

'Maybe we can see the houses and everything if we climb up there,' Linda whispered.

Jan shook his head. He wanted no more climbing of ladders. Suddenly he ran back to the yawning trap door in the floor. Down below lay darkness, a bottomless black hole. Jan stood petrified on the edge of the opening, staring down in horror at the floating darkness below him. He backed away; he turned and ran across the loft to the next ladder.

They laboriously climbed the next shaky ladder in the same way they had done before, Linda pressing on tightly behind Jan, her face almost pushing against Jan's wooden shoes. Then Jan lost one of his wooden shoes. It bounced off Linda's shoulder and clattered to the floor below. Jan started to cry—he wanted his shoe. But Linda didn't know how to go backward down the ladder. She kicked off both her shoes to make him feel better. Jan kicked off his other shoe.

They found they could climb much better in their thick woollen socks. But now Jan wanted to go back to get all the shoes. Linda pressed on. Jan had to climb.

Again there was only another loft when they pulled through the trap door, and again the windowlike opening was far too high for them to look out. They could not see the houses and the islands in the sea as Linda had promised. Jan began to sob bitterly. 'Linda had said . . .' For some reason Jan went stubbornly of his own accord to the next ladder and started to climb. Linda had to hurry up after him. The dry sobs pressed out of Jan like hiccoughs as he pulled himself through the next trap door. The last sob stopped in his mouth. Before him rose the enormous works of the tower clock. They had reached the clock loft!

The clock ticked at them. Jan stared round-eyed at the great coppery wheels and cogs. This time Jan urged Linda on. He was awed by the slow-moving wheels and the heavy ticking. There came a whirring high up in the machinery, and the clock struck one mighty bong. It was the half-hour.

'It hurt my ears when it bonged,' Jan said, delighted. He was amazed and thrilled. He grabbed hold of the iron framework as if to climb up into the works. Linda dragged him back.

'You mayn't. You mayn't go up there,' she said primly. 'Oh, will *your* mother . . .' She couldn't finish her threat. It reminded her of her own mother and of her own wrongdoing in going into the tower. 'Let's go up some more, *then* we'll see the islands,' she promised hastily, to get the guilty thought of her mother out of her mind.

'All right,' Jan said surprisingly. He was beginning to obey Linda as if she were his mother.

After Jan pushed himself through the trap door into the loft above, he stayed kneeling on the floor. 'What's that?' he said.

It was the bell! The great, enormous bronze bell that they had heard every day, all the days of their short lives. Now its size awed and astounded them. There it hung before them from thick beams in the ceiling. It was so large it barely cleared the floor.

Jan crawled to the bell and looked under it. There in the middle of the huge dome hung the big clapper. Jan suddenly lay down flat on his back and pulled himself by the rim of the bell to get under it and at the clapper. It fascinated him.

Linda stood staring at Jan's two feet. It alarmed her. Jan was under the bell! She grabbed his feet and tried to pull him back into view. Jan was immovable as he clung to the clapper.

'You've got to come out,' Linda cried desperately.

'I don't want to,' Jan yelled back. His voice came seeping out from under the bell so odd and muffled, it frightened Linda.

'Oh, Jan,' she quickly invented. 'You can see everything from here—the whole village and the roofs and *even* the islands.'

'I don't want to,' Jan said from under the bell.

'But you can even see *storks* flying in the sky,' Linda said.

She waited hopefully. She had heard so much about storks these last days that surely storks must be the ultimate in promises, something that would make Jan come sliding out. Jan did not bother to answer. His silence made Linda feel guilty. She had made it all up; she had fibbed! For the first time she took her eyes off Jan's protruding feet and looked around her guiltily, as if someone might have heard her fibs.

It was so! She hadn't fibbed! She *could* see out of the tower! Here where the great bell hung, the tower was open on three sides. Low openings, great big windowlike openings with slanting boards in them. She could peek between the boards, and there was the sky and the faraway sea and . . . and—even the islands! At one end of an island, a lighthouse rose white above the dark rolling sea.

But there were no storks.

Linda looked back at the bell. She wanted to call Jan out from there, but she had fibbed about the storks. She stared hard into the distances of the sea again as if to make storks happen. Her big sister, Lina, had talked about nothing but storks; she'd said there wouldn't be one stork left after the storm. Oh, but Lina had fibbed, too! There were storks. Two storks were coming over the sea! Two big storks, slow and flappy. Far away over the sea toward the lighthouse, just as white as the lighthouse. Now they were coming down. The storks had landed in the sea! They weren't flying any more. There they stood, far away, but not so far as the lighthouse. The storks stood in the sea!

Jan had to come to see them. Linda tiptoed to the bell, grabbed Jan's feet, and dragged him out before he had a chance to cling to the clapper.

'See! See!' Linda pointed the storks out to Jan. She even held his head between her hands so he'd look in the right direction.

'That white in the sea?' Jan asked. 'Two whites? Are they storks?'

'Yes. They were flying, but now they're just standing in the sea. I told you!'

'I see them.'

The motionless storks were hard to see, and motionless, they weren't fascinating very long. Jan went back to the bell to try to swing the big heavy clapper.

There was a knock on the schoolroom door, but before the teacher could reach the door, it flew open. Lina's and Auka's mothers stood there.

'Maybe we shouldn't . . .' Lina's mother started. 'Jan and Linda are gone! We've hunted all over the village.' Her voice was loud and desperate in the schoolroom. Her scared eyes sought out Lina. 'Lina, you've got to come. I don't know where to look any more.'

'You, too, Auka. Come,' Auka's mother said timidly. Then she began to cry.

'We'll all come,' the teacher said promptly. 'If we all take part we can go out in all directions.'

'We let them out at schooltime. We each thought they were next door at the other's house,' Auka's mother said helplessly.

Lina's mother nodded along with her. 'Linda— that's Lina's little sister—was talking about storks. She's heard Lina worry about the storks in the storm, and now we're afraid they went out into the country to look for storks. And the ditches brimful along every road! They're not in the village. I've been to every house.' She couldn't stand still any longer. She turned and ran out of the room. Auka's mother ran after her.

'I'll go with the women. A man along will make them feel better,' the teacher said hurriedly. 'Each of you take the same road you took to find a wheel. But two of you go along the sea and the dike.' He rushed out after the women.

It must be serious if the teacher dismissed school, Lina thought and bit her lip nervously. Jella did all the directing. She tagged mutely, almost gratefully, after him when he said, 'You and I'll take the dike, Lina.'

Jella walked fast along the top of the dike. Lina ran silently on behind him. The running on the wind-swept dike left her no breath for talk. She just let Jella talk. He seemed to feel important in being head of a scouting party. It wasn't his little sister who was gone! Jella in his importance seemed to lose sight of the reason they were on the dike. Now he was looking out to sea. 'We don't have to look for storks for the next few days,' he decided expertly. 'The storm is still blowing itself out over England.'

Lina felt scornful. Jella hadn't the slightest idea which way England lay. Jella was the worst at geography in the whole class! Then Lina felt anxious again and trotted faster. She wished it could have been Auka with her instead of Jella—Auka's little brother, Jan, was lost, too. Only then they'd both be too anxious. No, maybe it was better getting irritated by Jella, because then you thought other thoughts than the awful thought of Linda and Jan floating in a ditch full of water. Lina threw a hasty glance up at the tower clock—ten o'clock almost. Two hours Linda and Jan had been gone.

Jella had opinions on the tower, too. 'The teacher shouldn't have gone off with your mother and Auka's. He should have rung the bell. Then all the country people would come to the village, and they all could help look. Most likely if those two kids wandered into the country, somebody working on the land would have seen them.'

'Teacher couldn't do that!' Lina said hotly. 'He mayn't.' Why was she so irritated with Jella? 'You know the Government sets the times he must ring the tower bell. Why, they'd all come running, thinking something terrible had happened, like a fire or something.'

'Isn't this terrible enough?' Jella argued. 'Two little kids maybe drowned . . .' Oh, he shouldn't have said that, Jella realized too late. He heard Lina gasp. 'They'll be playing somewhere, locked up or something, you'll see,' he added hastily.

'Let's hurry,' Lina said.

They raced out of the village in the direction of old Douwa's turned-up boat. Just beyond the village the remnants of an ancient, dilapidated pier jutted a short way into the sea. All that was left of it was a row of jagged, uneven piles, sticking above the water like the worn teeth in an old man's mouth. But it was a temptation for children to crawl over the jagged piles to the pier's end. There were dangerous gaps in the pier and jagged holes where piles were missing.

Oh, but Linda and Jan were too young to go out on the pier and jump the gaps, Lina tried to reassure herself. She'd just thought the thought and there . . . She grabbed Jella's arm and stood pointing, speechless. Something white floated on the water in a gap between the piles. Something white. White! Oh, but the children wouldn't be wearing white—not in winter. It was awful how you scared when you were worried and anxious.

'It's nothing,' she managed to say. 'I thought I saw . . .' She didn't explain. Her relief left her body too limp for talk. 'Oh, it was nothing,' she gratefully said again.

Jella was still looking where she'd pointed.

'Nothing!' Jella said indignantly. 'It's storks, drowned storks!' He sprinted to the pier.

Lina couldn't run after him; her whole body felt loose and disjointed in her relief after her big scare. Oh, how that floating white had scared her! Jella had said storks! Lina found herself running. When she got to the foot of the row of piles, Jella was racing over them, jumping the gaps. Now he stretched long and flat and let himself hang down. They *were* drowned storks. One after the other Jella pulled them up by their dead wings and laid them on the piles.

A sombre Jella came slowly back to Lina, a stork dangling wet and lifeless from each hand. 'And Janus said . . .' Jella was almost crying. 'But it *was* the newspaper that was right! They drowned in the sea, and there won't be any storks. Come on, we've got to find the teacher, show him . . .'

'But Linda and Jan!'

194

'Oh, yes . . .' Jella looked down at the storks. 'Yah, that's right.' He stood torn between his duty and his need to show the teacher and the other boys his awful find. He half stooped as if to lay the two storks down on the dike. 'You go on,' he suddenly said. 'I'll run and find the teacher. I can run like anything—I'll come right back.'

He didn't wait. Holding the storks high by their long legs, he stormed up the dike and ran hard along the path. Lina stood staring forlornly after Jella. She half turned as if to go on alone. Her skirts fluttered in the wind. She could hear the lonely sound.

The finding of the dead storks, Jella's desertion, the loneliness of the sweep of windy dike and sea—it was all suddenly too much. She whirled and tore after Jella. 'Jella, wait! Jella!'

She sounded so sharp and shrill. Jella must have thought she had found Linda and Jan—maybe drowned, too. He stopped and then came running, the dead storks still in his hands. He stopped again and waited for Lina opposite the tower.

Now there was her sister, Lina, running back to that big Jella again. Jella had run away from her with the storks. But those weren't the storks that had come flying over the sea! Jella and Lina had gone and pulled the wrong storks out of the water. Linda, up in the tower, peered excitedly between the louvre boards of the big opening in the bell loft. 'Jella and Lina got two storks on the dike. And I see them!' she told Jan.

That made Jan come sliding out from under the bell. 'Where?' he asked even before he got to his feet.

'Oh, you've got to peek through the boards.' She pointed to the louvre boards.

Jan drew back.

'Don't be afraid.' Linda mothered him. 'Linda will hold you up.' She helped him climb.

195

Jan clung to the boards and peered down between them to the dike. 'Oh, I'm high,' he said, startled. He tried to scramble down, but Linda had both her hands against his back. 'I'm holding you,' she said encouragingly. 'Do you see them?'

'Yes, and they've got the two storks.'

'They haven't either,' Linda said indignantly. 'The other two are standing in the sea. Do you see them standing in the sea?'

'No,' Jan said.

It made Linda so impatient with Jan she decided she'd tell Lina. 'Lina,' she called from the tower. 'You've got the wrong ones.'

'Linda! Linda, where are you?' Lina's sharp call suddenly penetrated the high loft.

'I'm here!' Linda yelled back. The wind soughing between the slanting boards seemed to beat her words back at her.

'Where?' Lina yelled. 'Where, Linda? Tell me just where you are.'

'I'm up here, and Jan's gone back under the bell. Can't you see me?'

'Under the bell?' Lina's words came shrieking back. 'Are you way up in the tower?'

'Yes, and so is Jan.'

'Linda! Linda, is there a piece of stone up there? Go find a piece of stone and hit the bell with it. Hit it hard.'

Linda looked around the bell loft. There were all kinds of broken stones that had crumbled from the great walls. She picked up the biggest one. She had to lift it with both hands. She staggered to the bell with it. But when she tried to fling it against the bell, it just dropped; it was so heavy. It hit the rim of the bell before her toes—B O N G. A great, gross bong came roaring out of the bell. The sound swelled and circled and filled the whole loft. It scared Jan; he came squirming from under the bell. The sound still echoed all around them in the loft. Jan looked up, listening to it. He liked it; he was laughing. It frightened Linda. What had she done! She backed away as far from the bell as possible and ran against one of the openings in the tower.

'How did you do it, Linda? How did you make it bong?' Jan asked.

The awed Linda pointed to the big stone. Then Jan picked it up in both hands and hit the bell and hit it again—B O N G, B O N G. Everybody would hear it all over Shora!

'Now you did it!' Linda cried. 'Everybody heard it. Are *you* going to get it from *your* mother!' She pointed out of the board-covered opening as if to prove it.

It was so! In all the nearby fields people stood looking up at the tower. On some of the roads boys came running. Down one road came a man and two women, running toward the tower—the teacher and both their mothers! 'Now you did it,' Linda whispered. 'Here comes your mother.'

Jan started to cry.

Now Lina shouted from right below the tower, 'Jan and Linda, stay right there. Don't try to go down. The teacher is coming. Mother is coming.'

The teacher, both their mothers! Linda looked desperately around the loft. 'Your mother is coming, too,' she told Jan. 'Oh, you're going to get it. You rang the bell.'

'You did it first,' Jan wailed. He began to cry hard. Mouth wide-open, crying with all his might, he stumbled to the trap door. He took one horrified look through the opening and down all the ladders in all the deep lofts below. His crying died in his mouth. He backed away from the ladder, but when he turned, he saw the bell and began crying again. Linda cried with him.

197

They both were crying so hard, they did not hear the great iron door to the tower open far below them. They did not even hear the teacher and Jella coming up the rickety squeaking ladders until they were in the loft right below. Then it was too late to do anything. The teacher found them sitting side by side on the dusty floor, backs against the bell, crying with all their might.

'Well, well,' he said. 'What a high place to sit and cry and when there's nothing to cry about. Look, Jella's here, too, and Jella and I are going to carry you all the way down! Who wants to ride pick-a-back?'

Linda stopped crying and stretched her arms up to Jella, so that Jan would have to ride on the big, strange teacher's back. 'Just shut your eyes, and there'll be nothing to it,' the teacher said.

Linda obediently shut her eyes. All the way down the ladders she could hear the teacher coming on behind with Jan. The teacher was saying all kinds of nice things to Jan, but Jan just sobbed 'No' to all of the teacher's endless questions. Linda kept her eyes shut.

To Linda's amazement many people had gathered outside the tower. Everybody! And everybody was asking questions. Everybody was talking at one time. It was bewildering. Now her mother scooped her up and kissed her all over her dirty, dusty face. Jan's mother was doing it, too. And nobody was angry, and everybody was talking. Everybody was there, except the two white storks. They were lying on the dike. But how could she tell Lina in all this confusion and talk that they were the wrong storks? Her mother was hugging her so tight! And now her mother was carrying her home—like a baby. So was Jan's mother carrying him. All the others came on behind, even the teacher. How could she tell Lina anything? But she was ready at the first chance to tell Lina that she and Jella had gone and found the wrong storks.

CHAPTER XV

Storks
in the Sea

IT TURNED out to be little Jan who remembered to tell about the two storks that had flown down into the sea. His mother had carried him into the house, and now things were quieting down. Jan stood at the window to watch the big boys and Lina troop off to school to finish the interrupted morning session. The nice, quiet-spoken teacher, who had carried him down all the ladders, had told the big boys and Lina to get straight back to school. But Jella hadn't followed the teacher; he had run back to the dike. Jan knew what for! To get the storks! But Linda had said they were the wrong storks.

Jella had run off, but Auka had gone to the kitchen to get himself a slice of bread with syrup. Auka came hurrying through the house to run after the others. He was biting his syrup bread. There came Jella, too, far down the street with the two big storks.

'Look, Auka,' Jan called after his brother. 'He's got storks.'

'Storks?' Auka said. He stopped in his tracks. 'What are you talking about?'

199

'Jella's got storks, but he hasn't got the right storks, because the two live ones flew down in the sea. They stood in the sea.'

Auka wasn't even listening! He'd rushed to the window; he pulled the curtains aside. 'Dead,' Auka said in a queer voice, but he was talking to himself. 'Drowned in the storm.'

'Shall I show you where the other two storks are, Auka?' Jan said helpfully. He eyed Auka's slice of bread. Auka wasn't even eating it.

'What in the world are you talking about?' Auka said impatiently. 'Storks in the sea!'

'Honest, Auka.'

Auka looked hard at him. 'You're not just making this up?' he asked.

'Oh, no, Auka,' Jan said earnestly.

Jella was passing the house with the storks. Auka started to run out of the house after him. Then Auka turned to his younger brother. 'Does Linda know?' he asked.

'Oh, sure.'

Linda, being a little girl, knew ten times more words than Jan. Linda could explain herself. 'I'll go and ask Linda,' Auka said.

'May I have your bread, Auka? You're not eating it.'

'Here.' Auka handed it to his brother and hurried next door to question Linda.

'Oh, I forgot!' Linda said in amazement. To think she'd forgotten! 'I told Lina when I was in the tower, but she didn't hear me, and then I forgot. But two storks flew and flew, and then they flew down in the sea. I saw them, and I showed Jan. You can see them from the tower, Auka.'

Auka rushed out of the house. Jella was far down the street. 'Jella! Jella, come here. Come along with me. The kids saw storks fly down in the sea.'

'Sure, I've got them,' Jella hollered back.

'Live storks! They saw them fly. Hurry!'

Jella came sprinting. Halfway back to Auka, he took time to lay the storks down beside the steps of a house and then he came on again.

'They saw two storks come flying toward Shora—the way I make it out—and land in the sea,' Auka explained urgently. 'Maybe they landed somewhere on a sand bar. I don't know, but they say two storks were *standing* in the sea. Come on.'

The two boys raced to the dike. They searched the sea, but the dike wasn't high enough. They were just looking against the crests of leaping waves. In the distance where they knew the sand bar lay, they could see nothing but dark water.

Jella saw the dinghy which had been left behind by the fishing fleet. It rode restlessly at its short anchor rope below the dike. 'Let's take the dinghy and row out there.'

'In that kind of sea? Gosh, Jella, we can't just go out on the say-so of two kids.'

Auka looked at the tower. 'They were both so sure. Wonder if the teacher locked the tower door in all the excitement? He was carrying Jan.'

'You can see he locked the gate to the churchyard all right,' Jella said.

'Yes, but you're tall; you could boost me up over the churchyard fence. If I could get up in the tower . . .'

They raced down the dike to try the plan. Auka kicked his wooden shoes off, and Jella boosted him as high as he could up the woven wire fence. Auka could just barely grab the top of the fence. He clung there a moment; then with Jella giving a savage shove at his heels, he swung his legs high and managed to vault over the top. He barely cleared it. There was a ripping sound as he caught in the fence for a second. He fell down hard inside the churchyard. 'Made it,' he gasped. After giving his torn trousers a hasty glance, Auka picked himself up and dashed to the tower.

The door *was* unlocked. 'Wait there for me,' Auka yelled and disappeared inside.

Jella stood staring up at the tower until his neck ached. At last Auka's excited voice came from high in the tower. 'Jella, Jella, they're there! They're there! I saw them plain. One was flapping and struggling. Maybe they're sucked into the sand. Run and tell them at school. Tell Janus, too. And get the dinghy ready. Tell the teacher to open the gate for me. And . . .'

Jella wasn't listening to all the instructions. Jella was running hard.

Up in the bell loft Auka hurried to the ladder to go down, but then he had to look at the storks just once more. He stared hard at the tossing sea, and then he found the storks again. They were far out at sea, out toward the islands. Far behind them the lighthouse at the end of one island rose dimly white and round like a chalky crayon. The waves leaped grey and spooky under the dark sky. Only now and then, when the waves were levelled out before the sand bar, did the storks emerge from the greyness like two white blots. Then one stork began flapping its wings. The motion of its huge wings made it suddenly stand out clear. Amazingly, it rose and flew heavily above the sand bar. But its mate did not rise after it. The big stork flapped down again beside the other one. They stood side by side, lonely in the grey of the endless, restless sea.

Auka ran to the tower opening that overlooked the village. He stared over the roofs at the distant school. Nothing stirred there. They had to hurry! Ah, there was Janus now. There he came in the wheel chair down the empty street. A coil of rope was draped over the back of his chair. At the bottom of the dike, Janus sat helpless. The dike stopped him.

Janus looked up at the sky. Now his eyes turned to the tower clock. Auka guessed what he was doing—he was making a reckoning of the time for the flood tide to come. There couldn't be much time, for now Janus whirled his chair around impatiently and looked back down the street. There they came at last, the boys and Lina racing far out ahead of the teacher.

Janus did not wait for the teacher. He had the four boys carry him and his chair up the dike steps. Lina pushed with all her strength against the back of the chair. Now the teacher was there, too. He grabbed the chair with Lina. Up Janus went. Once on the top of the dike, he rolled himself headlong down the slope of the dike toward the sea. Oh, Janus knew. He was wasting no time. 'Good old Janus,' Auka said in his utter relief.

They were forgetting him! Auka started to yell at the group below the dike, but suddenly he reconsidered. It was far more important that they got the dinghy out.

Now Janus made Jella wade into the sea to bring the dinghy to the foot of the dike. Much water was standing against the dike even in the last hour of ebb tide. Big Jella wrestled the boat to the dike. Hey, they were lifting Janus into the boat—Janus himself was going out! That's why Janus had brought the rope. The teacher lashed Janus to the seat. Janus had thought of it, no one else would have. As he had no balance, Janus had to be tied down, otherwise, when he pulled on the oars, he'd go flat on his back into the bottom of the boat. Now Jella and the teacher got into the seat ahead of Janus's seat. Auka could see Janus handing the teacher a glove. Janus had even thought of that! But that was right, too. The teacher's hands were soft; without gloves they'd blister and be useless long before the hard pull to the sand bar was over.

Amazingly, Lina was going along, too. She was stepping into the back of the boat. And Pier! Pier clambered into the front! But Eelka and Dirk were staying behind. Why Pier and Lina? Oh, they were the smallest, the lightest—that must be it. Yes, that would be it. Pier and Lina were going along to hold the wild storks while the others rowed. Oh, Janus had thought of everything—good old Janus!

Now Eelka and Dirk were shoving the boat clear of the dike. Janus was flailing his oars mightily. Now the two in front were catching the rhythm of the oar stroke. The boat crept ahead and moved steadily away from the dike.

It would be a long hard journey. Auka hurried back to the sea side of the tower. When at last the waves let him see the storks again, the two white birds were standing like sentinels. They weren't flapping their wings any more. They weren't struggling.

Auka suddenly realized he was bone-cold. He shivered and hurried back to the village side of the tower to see what Dirk and Eelka were doing. They were running along the dike toward the tower, and Dirk was waving something. They had the key to the churchyard gate. Teacher hadn't forgotten him! Auka hurried down the ladders in the tower.

In the dinghy no one talked. The two men and Jella had to strain too hard at the oars for talk. The heavy work, the wash, and the unevenness of the fall and rise of the waves made it impossible for the inexperienced teacher to dip his oars in cleanly and pull at just the right time. He was doing his best, using every fibre of his untrained muscles. You couldn't ask more of the man. Janus bent his powerful body a little harder to the task of forcing the boat ahead.

Now and then, dipping in among the troughs and

rising on the crest of a wave, Lina in the stern could see Pier's head rise above the rowing men. Pier was keeping his eyes firmly fixed on the tower. Always when Pier's face bobbed up again, he was looking at the tower, never at the sea and the waves. His face was greenish, strained, but his lips were pale. Pier was fighting seasickness!

Even when riding the crest of a long wave, Lina could nowhere catch sight of the storks or the sand bar. The sea was an endlessly tossing mass; the sky was dark and sombre. Sometimes the tip of the lighthouse was pencilled white against the sky, then it sank into the sea again. Only Janus would know the distance to, and the exact location of, the sand bank, but Janus was grimly silent.

Suddenly he took his eyes off the two rowers ahead of him and flashed a look back at the tower and clock. He silently rowed on for a few minutes. 'Teacher,' he said impatiently, 'drop back. Crawl over to Lina and rest awhile.'

Without a word Jella slid into the centre of the seat the moment the teacher moved. He grabbed the teacher's oar. Janus began grunting and counting out a new rhythm he was setting to push the boat ahead harder. Jella fell into the rhythm at once. His powerful young back moved naturally in unison with the broad back of Janus. The four oars dipped and flashed together.

'You can see he's the son of a fisherman,' the exhausted teacher said to Lina.

Lina nodded. Her eyes searched the sea in the hope of finding something white among the grey waves.

Again Janus glanced back at the tower.

'Twenty minutes,' he muttered. 'In another twenty minutes the flood tide starts, and then we won't be going anywhere but back to the dike. And those storks will go under. Kid, if you ever rowed, row now.'

'Can we make it in twenty minutes in this sea?' the teacher asked.

'I'm setting a course that'll get us behind the sand banks,' Janus said. 'Once they're ahead of us, they'll break the force of the waves. It won't be so rough then, and we should make it.'

When Lina looked back again—she had made herself wait until she had seen Pier's head rise up twelve times—the face of the clock was blurry. They *were* moving. If you did it that way, you could see the progress. The boat wasn't just rising and falling and dancing. Janus and Jella were really pulling the boat ahead. Oh, they were strong. Pier kept his eyes away from the greenish waves and the water; he still looked only at the tower. The sweat was rolling down his sick face, but he stubbornly wasn't letting the seasickness get the best of him.

'Here we are,' Janus said at last, although it was noticeable to no one else. 'Now, Jella, ten more good strokes and we're in the lee of the banks. Come on, boy!'

At the end of the ten strokes, they all felt it, sensed it, although they could not really see it. But the great force of the waves seemed to be broken here. It was easy to tell that the boat forged ahead.

Without a word to anyone, the teacher crawled back to his seat at the oar. As the teacher started to row, there was a sudden rush and swirl of water. A swelling came to the whole sea. They rose, the whole sea rose. The ground swell of the tide had come. This was the beginning of the flood tide.

'The tide!' Pier yelled. They were the first words he had spoken.

'Now row!' Janus said fiercely. 'Row like mad. Chop it ahead.'

In a matter of seconds, the high back of a sand bar rose out of the water before them. Pier twisted around and stood up. Clinging with one hand to the side of the boat, he stretched as high as he dared to look over the sand bar for the storks.

Lina expected Janus to yell at him to sit down. But instead Janus told Pier, 'That's right, stand ready. Jump and run up that bank with the anchor the moment you think you can make it. Then go for those storks.'

Pier turned and stared at Janus in open-mouthed unbelief.

'That's right,' Janus yelled. 'That sand 's solid. I've been on it many a time. The real tide is just rolling in past the lighthouse right now. You've got time.'

The boat's bow shot up the bank and grounded in the sand. Pier jumped and landed hard with the heavy anchor. He held the anchor up against his chest and carried it part way up the bank where he dropped it. He looked to Janus for further instructions and assurance.

'You've got three minutes by my reckoning. In three minutes the flood tide will be rolling over this bank. Get going,' Janus said.

Pier looked scared, but he turned and scrambled up the bank. For a moment he stood on the top of the ridge. 'They're here! They're here!' he screamed. 'They're alive, but they're up to their necks in water.'

'Grab them,' Janus called hoarsely. 'Grab them by their necks and drag them here. They won't fight. They're done in. Quick now, kid, or you'll all three drown.'

With a last scared look at the boat, Pier disappeared. It was a tense, awful wait. The empty sand rose before them. Pier had vanished as if he'd sunk into the sea. Hidden from sight by the high ridge of sand but thunderous in their ears, the wall of flood tide water came rolling toward them in one great roar.

'It's coming,' Janus said. He dug his oar into the

sand and shoved the stern of the boat around so the boat would be lying broadside to the bank when Pier should come. 'Drag that anchor in. I'll hold the boat with the oar,' he called to Jella. 'Just get the anchor; don't you go over the ridge! That kid'll be lucky if he has time to make one jump for the boat. What's keeping him?'

Then from behind the ridge they heard a shout. 'Janus, Janus, the tide! Janus!'

Janus, forgetting himself, strained at the ropes as if to rise and run to Pier.

At that moment Pier's head appeared over the ridge. He came running wildly ahead of the roaring wall of water that seemed to thunder right behind him. He came plunging down the bank, his eyes horrified and huge. He was dragging two storks by their necks. Their wings flapped feebly.

'Jump, kid. Jump!'

Pier jumped. Lina caught one of the storks as it swung toward her. Pier crumpled into the bottom of the boat at her feet, still clutching the other stork. He lay there sobbing. 'They fought me. They wouldn't come. And they were so heavy and sunk in the sand,' he said over and over. Then he was suddenly angry. 'Janus, it *wasn't* solid! I sank in it, too, and the water came.'

Janus was too busy to answer. He ripped his oar out of the sand and pushed the boat free. The flood tide rushed over the sand bar like a hissing, seething waterfall. But the boat was free. Behind the bank the flood tide seized it and the boat shot ahead. Swiftly the boat was carried forward on the tide.

'I didn't make allowance for the storm,' Janus told Pier. 'Those five days of storm must have left all kinds of sticky sea silt on that sand. But you made it, didn't you?'

Lina sat with the stork in her lap. Pier crouched at

her feet, and a last sob forced its way out of him. He breathed deeply. He pulled himself up on the seat next to Lina and held the other stork in his lap. He and Lina sat very still. They sat looking at the great white birds, half-dead, half-drowned. Only a dim flicker in the eyes showed they were still alive. Pier softly stroked the long neck of his stork. Lina hugged her stork to her as if to warm it.

It was unbelievable—storks in their laps. Great, strange birds that flew over oceans and seas and continents were lying here in their laps. Pier and Lina looked at each other—an awed, astounded look—then they looked at the storks again, trying to believe it. They were unaware that the boat, riding rapidly out on the sweep of the tide, was nearing the dike and the tower.

'Hey, hold their necks!' Janus suddenly warned. 'They're still wild, even if they are pretty meek now. But with those bills they could knock holes in you two kids.'

Lina looked up alarmed. Pier didn't listen but went on stroking the long, stretched-out neck of the white bird for which he had almost given his life. It couldn't be believed.

'We've got two storks,' he mumbled queerly to Lina, as if only now was the fact beginning to dawn on him.

Suddenly Dirk, Auka, and Eelka were yelling at them from the dike. Pier and Lina looked up, startled. They were back! Here was the dike. And there stood not only Dirk, Eelka, and Auka but all the women and all the little children and Douwa; even Grandmother Sibble stood there. All of Shora was on the dike.

When Douwa had returned from his long walk to Ternaad and had come striding along the dike, Auka,

Dirk, and Eelka had shouted the good news to him, all three shouting at one time.

'Look,' Douwa told them when at last he understood what they were trying to tell him, 'look, we've got to assume that they'll make it back with the storks. With Janus there, they should make it. They'll be coming back with a couple of half-dead storks—but wild storks just the same. Those birds are not going to like being manhandled. So we've got to get ladders to the school and put those birds on their wheel the moment the boat lands. After that it will be up to the storks. My guess is that after what those poor beasts went through, they'll be so dead beat anything will look like home to them. The sooner we get them up on that wheel, the more likely they are to settle down and stay in Shora.'

Janus had ladders, they all knew. But Janus was out in the boat, and the shed where the ladders were stored was probably locked. They raced to Janus's house just the same, with Douwa, his stout stick tapping, walking sturdily behind them. The shed *was* locked.

'Break the door down,' Douwa ordered.

The three boys looked at him. Break into a shed that belonged to Janus!

Old Douwa chuckled. 'I'll take the responsibility. I don't think Janus will take me over his knee.'

When the boys still hesitated, Douwa himself marched up to the door. Using his stout stick as a crow bar, he inserted the tip of it under the hasp of the lock. The staple that held the hasp came squeaking out of the doorpost. Douwa went into the shed and the boys followed him. They hurried out with the ladders. The noise they made brought Grandmother Sibble III to her back door.

'I'd call that breaking and entering!' she called out from her back step. 'And, Douwa, at your age you ought to know better.'

'It's for a good cause, Sibble,' Douwa answered her.

'There's storks coming to Shora, Sibble. The first since you and I were kids, but these are coming by boat.' Over the high board fence Douwa explained the situation to the old lady. Her eyes sparkled.

'Now *that* I've got to see! For that I'll go up on that dike even if the wind blows me over—but I could use your stick, Douwa.'

Douwa handed his stick over the fence. 'You're getting old, Sibble.'

The boys were already far down the street with the two ladders.

'Well, I've got work to do,' Douwa said. He went back into the shed, came out with a coil of rope, and followed the boys. When Douwa arrived at the school, Dirk and Auka had already placed the first ladder against the wall of the school. Under Douwa's direction they carried up the second ladder and shoved it up on the roof. Douwa threw them the rope. They lashed the second ladder to the first and to the wagon wheel on the ridge of the roof.

The boys worked quickly. They were anxious to get back to the dike. Eelka had mysteriously disappeared. Now smoke belched out of the school chimney; bits of paper blew up and rained down on Dirk and Auka on the roof. 'What's he doing that for?' Dirk yelled at Douwa.

Eelka came out of the school, rubbing black hands and beating the peat dust off his trousers. He was proud to have thought of building a fire in the school stove. 'Those storks stood in cold water for hours after fighting all that storm. They may need some warmth to put life back in them,' he said.

'Well, well,' old Douwa said in surprise. 'What don't you kids think of—baking storks!'

Finally Dirk and Auka climbed down the ladders. The three boys immediately charged off toward the dike; old Douwa was unceremoniously left behind.

He marched after them. In the village street the two dead storks lying beside the steps of his own house caught Douwa's eye. He sternly called the three boys back. Dirk had to get two shovels out of Janus's shed. Auka and Eelka were sent off with the storks to the churchyard below the tower. When Dirk came with the shovels, Douwa made the boys dig a small grave just inside the gate of the churchyard.

'But should we do this on Government property?' Auka said doubtfully.

'We've done so much that's illegal the last hour, a little more won't hurt, I guess,' Douwa said, unconcerned. 'And who's to know?' He tipped his head toward the dike. All the women of Shora were gathered on top of the dike, all staring out at sea. The little children were with their mothers. Even old Grandmother Sibble III stood there, protected from the wind by the huddle of women.

'Oh, I wonder how they're doing,' Eelka said.

Douwa shrugged. 'You'll find out the minute you've got those storks buried. Can't leave dead storks lying around. If those two storks they're bringing in should start to fly around Shora and see the carcasses of their cousins, they might not feel so happy about Shora. They might want to get out as fast as they could.'

That was all that was needed. Auka and Dirk dug with a will, but they were too impatient to dig a very deep hole. After the storks were placed in the grave, the sod was replaced and trampled down. The boys could not wait another minute. They dropped their shovels and dashed to the dike. As old Douwa stooped to pick up the shovels, a great shout went up. Douwa let the shovels lie and went as fast as he could toward the dike. Everybody from the top of the dike had rushed down to the sea. Douwa mounted the crest just in time to see the three boys grab the sides of the dinghy and pull it close to the dike.

Lina jumped out with a stork in her arms. After her Pier came with another stork. They raced up the dike with the three boys jumping around them like eager dogs. Jella and the teacher had climbed out of the boat and now walked after the group. The women clambered up the dike.

Back in the boat Janus let out an enraged bellow. Everybody had forgotten him, tied down to his seat. 'Get that anchor up the dike, get that wheel chair down here, and get me out. Don't I count for anything round here any more?'

Old Douwa and the teacher went to Janus's rescue. The others marched over the top of the dike without so much as looking back. Grandmother Sibble was left behind, too, in the excitement.

In the group that set off for the school, no one had a thought for anything but the storks. Eelka, Dirk, and Auka were trying to tell Pier and Lina what they had done to get ready for the storks but kept interrupting themselves with eager questions about the storks. The five boys and Lina raced on. They left the women far behind. Still farther behind, the teacher and Douwa were inching the wheel chair down the dike. Janus sat fuming and raging, as eager and impatient as any of the children. 'I could have drowned or starved there in that boat, so long as those storks were all right,' he said.

'Calm yourself, Janus. You did your part,' Grandmother Sibble III told him. But she was doing her own level best, with the aid of Douwa's stick, to hurry before the wheel chair.

At the school Janus came into his own again. The whole group was waiting for him, uncertain whether or not to put the half-drowned, bone-cold storks up on the wheel or to warm them first in the schoolroom by Eelka's fire. They shouted the perplexing question at Janus.

Janus made them wait until his wheel chair had been pushed right among them. Then he had to consider for a maddeningly long time. 'Well, if I was a stork, and had just come out of Africa, and had a storm knock the stuffing out of me for five days and nights, and on top of that had sat on a cold sand bar with the water spitting me in the eye . . . If I was a stork, I'd want to sit *on* that stove.'

Lina and Pier immediately carried the storks inside. Janus was the authority. Chairs were hastily shoved near the stove for Pier and Lina. They seated themselves and held the storks carefully in their laps.

'What did I tell you? Get one hand around those necks!' Janus suddenly bellowed from the doorway. 'When those fellows come alive, they could peck your eyes out.'

'You carried them all the way,' Auka and Eelka were begging Pier and Lina, 'now let us hold them a while.' Lina looked so tight-lipped and stubborn, they centred their attention on Pier. 'Come on, Pier!' Dirk said. 'If you can't even let your own brother——'

'Let him alone, all of you,' Janus told them fiercely. 'He risked his neck to get them off that sand bar.'

Lina sat quietly, looking down at her stork. She had to hold herself very quiet, absolutely still, or she'd burst out and scream and laugh and cry. It was so unbelievable, so wonderful, sitting in school with a stork in her lap. Storks in school, storks in Shora! She bent deep over her stork and cried a little and stroked its long, white neck.

Behind Lina, old Douwa was explaining to Janus what they had done to get ready for the storks—how they'd broken into Janus's shed and used his ladders, rope, and shovels. Janus did not seem to be too attentive. When the teacher, standing beside him, heard about the burial of the storks in the churchyard, he was shocked. 'But, Douwa, it's Government land!

That's against the law. That's punishable. It belongs to the State and the Queen.' He was scandalized. 'They'll have to come out of there.'

Janus twisted his wheel chair to face him. 'So it's Government property, so they dug a little hole, so the Queen won't like it! Well, let the Queen come and dig them up and drag them off to Amsterdam and bury them behind the palace!'

Janus suddenly realized what he was saying. He guffawed. The picture of the Queen dragging the storks down all the roads to Amsterdam and digging a little hole behind the palace filled him with delight. He roared with laughter.

Everybody tried to quiet him. 'Janus, the storks! You'll scare the storks!'

'Huh,' Janus said. 'If they're used to lions roaring all around them, they won't mind Janus.' He threw his head back again to laugh.

At the stove Lina's stork struggled in her arms, struggled wildly. Its long neck and wild eyes rose high above her. Janus's laugh stopped in his mouth. 'Grab him, Jella! Grab that neck,' he cried. 'And up with them on the wheel. Quick! Now that the blood's running in their veins again. Come on, Pier!'

Pier and Jella jumped to his orders. They remembered Janus's cautioning and kept a hand around the long necks. The stork under Jella's arm struggled wildly, trying to twist free from his grasp.

'Don't choke him, you young idiot,' Janus said sternly.

Up on the ladder Jella had to let go his hold on the stork's neck; he needed both hands to climb the ladder. With the big stork tucked under one arm, he climbed up. Pier followed right behind him. On the roof they had to crawl slowly along the ladder. Suddenly Jella's stork began fiercely pecking at his head. Jella closed his eyes and let him peck. The sharp jabs

215

knocked off Jella's cap. The stork's hard bill hammered down on his bare head. A tuft of hair came away in his bill. Jella squealed. He could take no more. He braced himself against the ladder, grabbed the stork with both hands and tossed him up toward the wheel.

Big white wings opened. Jella's stork landed on the rim of the wheel. Pier handed his stork to Jella who reached high to place the stork on the wheel. Stretching his long neck down, the big male stork angrily pecked at Jella. Jella hastily released his mate. The male stepped over and stood above her defensively. Slowly her head lifted, her long neck came up, she looked at her lord and master.

'Loosen that rope and down with the ladders,' Janus called from below. 'While they're still all in. Later it might scare them away.'

Jella lay flat on the ladder as he untied the knot in the rope underneath the wheel. Everybody helped to pull the ladders down. They laid them along the school wall. Then all retreated to the road and stood, without speaking or moving, staring up at the two storks on the wheel. The male stork stood tall and white, looking down at them. His mate had gathered her legs under her and sat squat against the hub of the wheel.

The male stork circled the wheel with slow, stately steps, studying it and now and then tapping the rim with his bill. When he had completed his inspection of the wheel, he stood tall and dignified again, looking up at the sky. His long bill opened and he began making hard clapping sounds up into the sky. The female tilted her head and listened; she struggled to get to her feet.

The male gently ran his bill along her white neck. Suddenly he spread his wings and flew down from the roof. He landed in the playground, right before the

hushed crowd gathered in the road. His sharp eyes had seen a long twig. He seized it in his bill. Flapping his wings heavily in his weariness, he rose to the roof and dropped the twig on the wheel before his mate. Gravely he bowed before her and pushed the twig closer to her. Still sitting in her exhausted huddle, she touched the twig with her bill and drew it toward her. She seemed to accept the twig as a promise of the nest they were going to build there. The male stork settled down on the wheel close beside her and closed his eyes.

Down in the road nobody said a word. The little group stood silent, staring up at the roof of the school. Then Janus whispered, 'They've shown us they're grateful. They've shown they're going to stay and build their nest. Now let's all quietly get away from here and leave them alone.'

They tiptoed away, solemnly turning to look back at the storks, and Janus rode in their midst.

'You can't believe it,' Janus kept whispering. 'You can't believe it—storks in Shora.'

'Not since I was a little child,' Grandmother Sibble III said softly to herself.

'Storks in Shora,' Lina repeated. 'But I can believe it, Janus! It's so impossibly impossible, I can believe it now.'

'Ah, yes, little Lina,' the teacher said. 'So impossibly impossible that it just had to be. And the long dream —storks on every roof in Shora—is beginning to come true.'

TITLES IN THE NEW WINDMILL SERIES